Father Edmund of the Heart of Mary

Passion Flowers

Father Edmund of the Heart of Mary

Passion Flowers

ISBN/EAN: 9783337812119

Printed in Europe, USA, Canada, Australia, Japan

Cover: Foto ©Thomas Meinert / pixelio.de

More available books at **www.hansebooks.com**

Faithfully yours in Xt,

Edmund, C.P.

PASSION FLOWERS

BY

FATHER EDMUND OF THE HEART OF MARY, C.P.
[BENJAMIN D. HILL]

Author of " A Short Cut to the True Church ; or,
The Fact and the Word "

NEW YORK, CINCINNATI, CHICAGO

BENZIGER BROTHERS

PRINTERS TO THE HOLY APOSTOLIC SEE

1898

PREFACE

Twenty years ago I published a small volume of " Poems, Devotional and Occasional." Friends to whom they are familiar have been joined by readers of the *Ave Maria*, as also by litterateurs of well-merited reputation, in urging me to bring out a fresh collection.

After much delay (for my life is a busy one), I am complying with this request. The poems above mentioned will be found in the present collection, but many of them revised and improved: and some will appear in each of the three sections, or volumes, into which this new issue is divided.

I am printing but one volume at a time. The first is entitled " Passion Flowers," as consisting of lyrics and sonnets either in honor of Our Divine Lord's Passion, or connected with it or referring to it : together with a narrative poem in two parts — " St. Hermenegild : a Passion Flower of Spain."

5

The second volume will be called " Mariæ Corolla " — that is, " A Wreath for Mary "; and will contain pieces either directly or indirectly in honor of Our Blessed Lady. My reason for choosing the Latin title will be given in an introduction to the book itself.

The third volume will comprise " Poems of Affection and Friendship." Perhaps it will have a classic title, like its predecessor. Under the head of " Friendship " will be found " Letters to An Old Chum," and pieces of a humorous kind.

I am well aware that the literary path I have chosen is not one that leads to popularity — in the wider sense of the term. It would, doubtless, have been more " worldly wise " — and, certainly, very much easier — to fall into line with the revived Pagan morality and the worse than Pagan scepticism of the day. If " I wish," as Wordsworth said of himself, " to be considered as a teacher, or as nothing," why not pose as an agnostic or a pantheist ? Why not dress up the " creed of despair " in a new and fascinating garb — as certain novelists have done ?

Because, by God's grace and undeserved mercy, I believe in Him; and in the truths of Christianity as revealed by Him; and in the Catholic Apostolic Roman Church as the only historical and logical Christianity. I therefore humbly offer to this Church whatever I have been able to produce with the talent committed to my charge. I aspire to teach with lyre and lute, as well as from the pulpit or with pen of solemn prose.

And having made poetry a study for thirty years, I ought to know the difference between mere religious verse and the beauties of our holy Faith set forth in poetic raiment.

If I have a model at all, it is dear old Horace — faultless master of poetic form. There is neither affectation nor obscurity in *him*. Those were not considered charms in the age of classic lore. Accuracy and strength were the combination that made golden Greek and golden Latin. To be sure, we find " bold constructions " in Sophocles and in Horace: a fact which makes these authors the best test of scholarship. But they never aimed at appear-

ance of depth by concealing, instead of express-
ing, their thought.

Again, I acknowledge, of course, the influence
of Tennyson, who triumphantly established his
right to introduce a new school of English
poetry. He, like Horace, is a master of scholarly diction; and, in a word, the most *perfect*
of English poets. He has been even called
" faultless to a fault." Yet he does not escape
occasional obscurity — the result of excessive
subjectivism. Some of his imitators take this
blemish for a beauty. I trust that I am not
among them.

Byron and Moore, the idols of my youth, are
certainly far from being models of style, by
reason of their inaccuracy — defect of scholarly
diction: but the strength of the one and the
simplicity of the other have never been sur-
passed, if equalled; and their influence abides
with the mind that has loved and studied them.
In the present volume, to some extent, but
more in the second and third, their influence
— particularly that of Byron — will be recognized, no doubt. And I am not at all ashamed
of it.

I must add a few words about the sonnet —
a form of composition to which I am very
partial.

When I began to write "quatorzains," I did
not know that the sonnet of Petrarch set up for
being the only correct one. I have adhered to
that form in my "Sonnets on the Way of the
Cross," which I deem my best work in the
present volume; but have not kept exclusively
to it since, and do not mean to do so in the
future. I believe the English language impor-
tant enough to have a sonnet of its own. The
Shakspearian form is duly recognized. But
Wordsworth is incomparably the greatest com-
poser of the sonnet that our literature can boast
of; and he varies not only the " minor system,"
but often the " major " too, and in a way that
suits the genius of the English language. So,
too, with Keats, that young giant of song,
whose sonnets are among our very finest. I am
quite content, then, to err in such company —
if error there be in my theory.

In closing this long preface, I beg to acknowledge the kindness of the editors of the

Ave Maria, the *Catholic World, Donahoe's Magazine,* the *Messenger of the Sacred Heart,* the *Rosary Magazine,* and the *Poor Souls' Advocate,* in allowing me to reprint poems contributed to their pages. The great majority of pieces now collected, and which were not collected in 1877, have appeared in the *Ave Maria.* Some, however, are now published for the first time : notably, " St. Hermenegild."

ST. MARY'S RETREAT, DUNKIRK, N.Y.
Feast of St. Rose of Lima, 1897.

CONTENTS

PART I

From 1866 to 1878

Part II

From 1878 to 1897

Contents

SAINT HERMENEGILD

A Passion Flower of Spain

PART I

FROM 1866 TO 1878

LOVE'S PRISONER

REPOSING in His altar-home —
　　Imprison'd there for love of me —
My Spouse awaits me; and I come
　　To visit Him awhile, and be
A solace to His loneliness —
If aught in me can make it less.

But is He lonely?　Bend not here
　　Adoring angels, as on high?
Ah, yes : but yet, when we appear,
　　A softer glory floods His eye.
'Tis earth's frail child He longs to see;
And thus He is alone — for me!

His Heart, how piningly it aches
　　With love unheeded, love despised!
O happy soul, that comes and takes
　　The gift as something to be prized :
The lavish graces it receives
From that full breast its prayer relieves!

Then, best of lovers, I'll draw near
    Each day to minister relief.
For tho' the thought of year on year
    Of sin should make me die of grief,
Yet day by day my God I see
" Sick and in prison " — all for me !
1866.[1]

----◆----

ST. MARY MAGDALEN OF PAZZI

TO THE SACRED HEART

"I say, my Jesus, Thou art *mad* with love ! I say so, and
shall always say so." — St. Mary Magdalen of Pazzi.

HEART of hearts, a love is Thine
    Madly tender, blindly true !
Love in vastness so divine,
    In excess so human too !
Seems it more a burning grief —
Pining, aching for relief.

Seems Thou dost not, canst not live,
    Save to sue us for Thy rest :
While the all that we can give

[1] The year of the author's conversion to the Faith.

Is as nothing at the best.
Wondrous Lover! shall I say
Thou hast thrown Thyself away?

Drench'd with anguish — steep'd in woe —
    Thou must needs, insatiate still,
Linger patiently below,
    Prison'd to Thy creatures' will:
While the current of the days
Murmurs insult more than praise!

Here I find Thee, hour by hour,
    Waiting in Thy altar-home,
Full of mercy, full of power —
    Mutely waiting till we come:
Waiting for a soul to bless —
Some poor sinner to caress.

Forth, then, from the fragrant hush,
    Where I almost hear Thee beat,
Bid a benediction gush —
    O'er me, thro' me, thrilling sweet!
Heart of Jesus, full of me,
Fill mine — till it break with Thee!

OUR BETHLEHEM

BETHLEHEM, House of Bread,[1]
  Of the Bread that came down from heaven.[2]
  " For the life of the world 'tis given :
Eat of it," Jesus said.

" Father," He bade us pray,
  " Give us this heavenly bread "
  (" Ours " we must call it, He said) :
" Give us it day by day."

Knelt in the midnight cave
  The shepherds and sages three,
  Theirs (do we envy ?) to *see*
The Bread which the Father gave.[3]

We in the Faith's broad day
  Kneeling — nor once, but at will —
  Take of that Bread our fill,
None " sent empty away."

How should *we* envy *them ?*
  Yet as the grace, the shame,
  If but in boast we claim
The goodlier Bethlehem.

[1] The literal signification of Bethlehem.
[2] St. John vi. 33, 51, 52.   [3] Ibid. v. 32.

OUR EPIPHANY

WHAT tho' we cannot, with the star-led
    kings,
Adore the swaddled Babe of Bethlehem,
Behold how sweetly Benediction brings
    A new Epiphany denied to them.
The Mary Mystical 'tis ours to see
    Still from His crib the little Jesus take,
And show Him to us on her altar-knee,
    And sing to Him to bless us for her sake.
Shall we the while be kneeling giftless there?
    In loving faith a richer gold shall please;
A costlier incense in the humblest prayer;
    Nor less the myrrh of penitence than these.
And there between us holy priesthood stands,
Our own St. Joseph, with anointed hands.

———◆———

ST. JOSEPH'S MONTH

SAINT of the Childhood and the Hidden
    Life,
    Why is it that thy month is always Lent?

What hadst thou with the Passion ?   Mary
    went
To Calvary with Jesus ; but the knife
Of that fierce sorrow was spared thee.   Thy
    strife
  In anxious care and fostering patience spent :
  Now to a stable, now to Egypt sent,
And then long years with humblest labor rife.
But this thy portion of the coming Cross —
  Which o'er thy path its forward shadow threw.
    And is not ours like thine — to walk content
In that long shadow, counting all things loss
  Save what for Jesus we endure or do ? —
    To teach us *this* thy month is always Lent.

THE PASSION

WAS ever tale of love like this ?
    The wooing of the Spouse of Blood :
Who came to wed us to His bliss
  In those eternal years with God.

Those griefless years, those wantless years,
  He left them — counting loss for gain —

To taste the luxury of tears,
    And revel in the wine of pain!

'Twas sin had mixt the cup of woe
    From Adam pass'd to every lip:
And none could shirk its brimming flow —
    For some a draught, for all a sip:

When Jesus came, athirst to save;
    Nor sucked content a sinless breast;
But grasped the fatal cup, and gave
    That Mother half, then drained the rest.

Enough the milk without the wine.
    When first the new-born Infant smiled,
'Twas merit infinite, divine,
    To cleanse a thousand worlds defiled.

But *we* must take of both.   And how
    Could love look on, nor rush to share?
Or hear us moan: "Death's darkness now:
    And Thou, at least, wast never there"?

And so He drank our Marah dry:
    Then filled the cup with wine of heaven.

Who would not live — with Him to die ?
Or not have sinned [1] — when so forgiven ?
LENT, 1872.

———◆———

THE FEAST OF THE CROWN OF THORNS

MY Thorn-crown'd King, Thy diadem
Outshines the bard's, the hero's, wreath.
The tangled gold, the ruby gem,
How fair they glitter underneath !

And ah, those gems ! They flow — they fall !
The dust receives them ! Shall they lie
Unheeded there ? O no ! They call
Adoring legions from the sky.

Yet not for Angels do they flow :
For sinful men. " And one is mine,
Dear Lord — my very own ? " . . . But lo !
His eyes reproach me : " All are thine."

---

[1] This, of course, is in the sense of the Church's " O felix
culpa ! O certe necessarium peccatum ! "

TO THE FIVE WOUNDS

DEAR Wounds, it is not mine to see you bleed
  As Magdalen saw you.   Where He reigns
    above
You shine in glory.   Yet, in very deed,
Remain, as then, five rosy mouths — to plead
  With Him for mercy, and with me for love.

" Behold upon My Hands I have graven thee !"[1]
  Indelibly, my King.   How sweet the thought!
Thou canst not look on these but reading me :
Thy Father there, Thy Mother too, must see
  What less my sins than Thy dear love have
    wrought.

Yea, Lord, and on Thy Feet — those blessèd Feet
  Where Magdalen's pure tears and kisses fell.
Ah, could mine own that homage now repeat
Of wordless thankfulness — if such were meet
  For sinner rescued from a lower hell !

And on Thy Side, my Jesus — ay, Thy Heart !
  And deepest there.   Right to the centre went

[1] Is. xlix. 16.

The soldier's spear: to show, with cunning art,
How *Thy* love giveth not itself in part,
   But all, my God!—with naught but all con-
      tent.

Sweet Wounds, then, home me! Hide me
         evermore
From sin and self! I ask to live and die
Hidden in you; for there is all my store
Of wisdom as of merit. Other lore
   Than that you teach shall pass unheeded by.

———◆———

THE STATIONS OF THE CROSS

I

'TIS thou, my cruel heart, but thou
      Hast wrought the doom thou weepest now.
'Tis thou hast shouted, " Let Him die!"—
Thy every sin a " Crucify!"
" I die," He murmurs, " die for thee:
Then sin no more: live true for Me."

II

Why choose a death of fierce delay
To agonize Thy life away?

And why do Thy embraces greet
The cross as if Thou deem'st it sweet?
Thou dost!   A sateless love, we know,
Must ever glut itself on woe.

III

Thou fallest — all too weak!   The might
That bears creation's infinite
As tho' its myriad worlds were none,
Has sunk beneath the sins of one!
Ye ruthless stones, thou heedless sod,
How can ye wound your prostrate God?

IV

They raise Him up, and goad Him on;
When lo, the Mother meets the Son!
How heart rends heart, as eye to eye
Darts the mute anguish of reply!
Sweet Lady, traitor tho' I be,
Yet let me follow Him with thee!

V

The soldiers fear to see Him die
Too soon for cross and Calvary;
And the Cyrenian, captive made,
Reluctant lends his timely aid.

O happy Simon, didst thou know!
Give me the load thou scornest so!

VI

Who calls that face unlovely now,
For furrowed cheek and thorn-pierced brow?
To me it never seemed so fair;
For when was love so written there?
Kind Veronica, get me grace
To keep, like thee, that pictured face![1]

VII

Again He falls! again they deal
Their ruffian blows — those hearts of steel!
He hails His Mother; and the throng
Slink back, to let her pass along.
She kneels to soothe Him and caress,
And rage grows dumb at Her distress.

VIII

The tender women mourn His fate,
With Mary's grief compassionate.
How blest such mourners, He has said:
They shall indeed be comforted.

[1] Our Lord left the impression of His face on St. Veronica's
cloth.   This relic of the Passion is still preserved in Rome.

And He, in turn, has tears for them —
Daughters of lost Jerusalem.

IX

And yet another fall! Ah, why?
'Tis my repeated perfidy.
O Jesus, I but live in vain
If only to be false again!
O Mary, grant me, I implore,
To die this hour, or sin no more!

X

The Way, the lingering Way, is past,
And Calvary's top is gained at last.
With gall the soldiers mock His thirst,
Then strip Him, in their glee accurst.
Descend, ye Angels! round Him flame,
And with your pinions veil His shame!

XI

Ah see, they stretch Him on the wood:
The blunt nails spurt the Precious Blood!
Nor His alone their every sting;
For Mary hears the hammers ring.
Lord, let that sound my music be
When the death-hour shall strike for me!

XII

A horror wraps the earth and sky
While three long times go darkly by.
And now, "'Tis finished!" Jesus cries:
And awfully the God-Man dies.
My heart, canst thou survive content?
Behold, the very rocks are rent!

XIII

Desolate Mother, clasping there
Thy lifeless Son, yet hear my prayer!
Tho' never was a grief like thine,
And never was a guilt like mine,
Still should I not be dear to thee
When He thou lovest died for me?

XIV

His lovers lay Him in the tomb,
And leave Him to its peaceful gloom.
Thou sleepest, Lord, Thy labor done;
For me — for all — redemption won:
And I, in turn, as dead would be,
And buried to all else but Thee.

LENT, 1870.

"THOU ART GONE UP ON HIGH" [1]

"GONE UP!" But whither?   To a star?
    Some orb that seems a point of light,
Or one too infinitely far
    For our fond gaze beneath the night?

Some fairer world, to which our own,
    With all its vastness, is a grain?
Is't there the God-Man sets his throne —
    Fit centre of a boundless reign?

Let science coldly sweep away
    A fancied Eden here and there
From out the starry space, and say
    'Tis *all* brute matter — crude and bare:

Or stern philosophy demand
    " May not yon myriad orbs we ken
Be but a pinch of golden sand
    To stretch the narrow minds of men?" —

Yet faith makes answer, meekly bold:
    " Narrow to me your widest lore —
Without the blessèd truth I hold
    That God is Man for evermore.

1 " Ascendisti in altum." — Ps. lxvii.

" He came to wed our life to His:
  As Man was born, and died, and rose:
And in His victor Flesh it is
  Our hopes of Paradise repose.

" He wore it thro' the sweet delay
  That kept Him with His dear ones yet;
Nor put it from Him on the day
  He pass'd from topmost Olivet.

" Then still He wears it in the skies —
  Matter in space.   And when the cloud
Receiv'd Him from the gazers' eyes —
  Before their brimming hearts allowed

" That they had lost Him — swift as thought,
  He reach'd the bright elysian home
His own primeval word had wrought,
  New Eden for the race to come."

HYMN [1]

NOT ours to ask Thee " What is truth ? "
  For here it shines the light of light:

[1] Written to be sung at the meetings of a "Christian Doctrine
Society" under the patronage of St. Paul.

And all may see it, age or youth,
  Who will but leave the outer night.
'Tis ours to tread, not seek the way
That brightens to the perfect day.[1]

But this we ask Thee, dearest Lord:
  Let faith, so precious, feed and grow;
And make our lives the more accord
  With fear and love, the more we know:
For thus, too, shall we point the way
That brightens to the perfect day.

Nor have we learnt it save to teach:
  It is for others we are wise:
The humblest has a charge to preach
  Thy kingdom in a nation's eyes:
A nation groping for the way
That brightens to the perfect day.

O thou, our Patron, great St. Paul,
  Apostle of the West! to thee
We boldly come, and fondly call,
  As children at a father's knee:
Come thou, and with us lead the way
That brightens to the perfect day!

[1] Prov. iv. 18.

ORDINATUS

THE priest, " another Christ "[1] is he,
    And plights the Church his marriage vows:
Thenceforth in every soul to see
    A daughter, sister, spouse.

Then let him wear the triple cord
    Of father's, brother's, husband's care:
In this partaking with His Lord
    What Angels cannot share.

O sweet new love!   O strong new wine!
    O taste of Pentecostal fire!
Inebriate me, draught divine,
    With Calvary's desire!

"I thirst!" He cried.   The dregs were drained:
    But still "I thirst!" His dying cry.
While one ungarner'd soul remained,
    The cup too soon was dry.

Yet what if *I* be crucified,
    And scoffing fiends, when all is done,
Make darkness round me, and deride
    That not a soul is won?

[1] "Sacerdos alter Christus." — St. Bernard.

God reaps from very loss a gain;
  And darkness here is light above.
Nor ever did and died in vain
  Who did and died for love.
1871.

———◆———

"SICUT MAGISTER EJUS"[1]

THE Priest must bear the Master's cross
  Of all men most, and take his part
In hours of failure and of loss
  Like those which wrung the Sacred Heart.

Yet, doubly sure, are others given,
  Of such sweet comfort, it is worth
The rest to know them: as, in heaven,
  A moment compensates for earth.

———◆———

TO ST. MARY MAGDALEN

'MID the white spouses of the Sacred Heart,
  After its Queen, the nearest, dearest
    thou:

[1] "It is enough for the disciple that he be as his Master." —
St. Matt. x. 25.

Yet the auréola around thy brow
Is not the virgins' — thine a throne apart.
Nor yet, my Saint, does faith-illumined art
   Thy hand with palm of martyrdom endow:
   And when thy hair is all it will allow
Of glory to thy head, we do not start.
O more than virgin in thy penitent love!
   And more than martyr in thy passionate woe!
     Who knelt not with thee on the gory sod,
How should they now sit throned with thee
     above?
   Or where the crown our worship could be-
     stow
     Like that long gold which wiped the feet
     of God?
1872.

FOR THE GIFT OF TEARS

MY Magdalen, my own dear Saint,
   Could I but weep my past away
   Like thee at Jesus' feet, the day
He cleansed thy bosom of its taint!

It is not, Sister, that I doubt
   Forgiveness.   He is all too sweet.

Had I too bathed and kissed His feet,
And heard Him say 'twas blotted out,

I scarce were more assur'd than now :
   For grace on grace has bid me cease
   From fearfulness, and " go in peace,"
With youth renewed in heart and brow.

Yet, by that fire of deathless love,
   Which, kindled at His glance and word,
   Consumed thee for thy Saviour Lord,
As burn the Seraphim above:

By all His tenderness, and those
   Divinely-human looks and ways :
   The thrilling sweetness of His praise,
The joy of mutual repose :

By all the darkness and the scorn
   Of those three hours beneath His cross :
   By all thy share in Mary's loss,
And, happier, in her Easter morn :

Get me the precious gift of tears,
   To flow perennial as thine !
   Thy prayer, dear Saint, shall make them mine,
And wreathe with gems my rescued years.

"JUXTA CRUCEM"

"DEAR Lord," we say, " could we have stood
    With Thy sweet Mother and St. John
      Beside Thy Cross; or knelt and clung
    (Heedless what ruffian eyes look'd on)
      With Magdalen's wild grief, and flung
Our arms about th' ensanguined wood!" . . .

But have we not the Crucified
    Among us, " even at the door"?
      Whom else behold we day by day
    In the sore-burden'd, patient poor?
      And where disease makes want its prey,
Can we not stand *that* cross beside?

O blest vocation, theirs who come,
    At chosen duty's high behest,
      To soothe the squalid couch of pain
    With pledges of a better rest
      Than all earth's wealth can give or gain,
And whispers of eternal home!

Never so near Our Lord as then,
    We touch *His* wounds — more heal'd than
        healing:

Never so close to Mary's Heart,
Hear too for *us* its throbs appealing :
And when for other scenes we part,
It is with John and Magdalen.

———◆———

TRANSPLANTED

WHO says she has wither'd, that little white
rose ?
She has been but removed from the valley of
tears
To a garden afar, where her loveliness glows
Begemm'd with the grace-dew of virginal
years.

I knew we should lose her. The dear Sacred
Heart
Has a nook in earth's valley for flowerets so
rare ;
And keeps them awhile in safe shelter, apart
From the wind and the rain, from the dust
and the glare ;

But all to transplant them when fairest they
bloom,

When most we shall miss them.   And this,
 that our love
May be haunted the more by the fadeless perfume
 They have left us to breathe of the Eden
 above.

Farewell, happy maiden !   Our weariest hours
 May gather a share of thy perfect repose.
And fragrantly still with the Lord of the flowers
 Thou wilt plead for thy lov'd ones — our
 little St. Rose !

A MEMORY

I LITTLE took her for a wife.
 She seem'd to stand, with maiden grace,
 Half eager, half averse, to face
The stern realities of life.

But when her tale of bitter wrong
 Had pierced me (tho' her words were few),
 I read her as myself, and knew
How old the heart with such a song.

And yet not quench'd its vital youth,
 Or blighted with a hopeless doom.
 " A flower," I said, " reserv'd to bloom
In sunshine of the future truth.

" She droops, nigh broken, in the night —
 So burden'd with the rain of woe :
 But each big drop gives purer glow,
And gems her for the dawning light."

———◆———

TO A LADY

ON THE DEATH OF HER SISTER

HER death is as of one I knew.
 Nor only that a friend's distress
 Is mine. Your sister, could I less
Than picture her another *you?*

She led, you say, an angel's life
 Ere ever the dividing vows
 Had wed her to the Virgins' Spouse
And seal'd her for the higher strife.

A chosen soul, then, from her birth ;
 Predestined to the perfect flower :

First gather'd for the convent-bower,
Now for a garden not of earth.

You know it, lady; and the sense
    Forbids the natural tear to flow,
    Unless a joy be with its woe
To give it thankful eloquence.

Nor have you lost her. Veil'd before,
    And cloister'd in a distant home,
    She now is free again to come
And linger near you evermore :

And shield you in a thousand ways,
    And guide your path, and plead your cause :
    For so the beatific laws
Of heaven work their Maker's praise.

And this I wish you, dearest friend :
    To catch her mantle with its fold
    Of fragrance and its clasp of gold,
And wear it to as sweet an end.
    1869.

TO THE SAME

MY wish is granted. You have caught
  Your sister's mantle, as I prayed:
Nor any friend is happier made
Than he who weaves this tribute thought.

This Mary takes " the better part ";
  And walks secure in her retreat,
  Where softly falls about her feet
The shadow of the Sacred Heart:

A shadow and a sunshine too —
  A light, a fragrance, and a rest:
  A peace like that which keeps the blest,
And " inly kisses thro' and thro'."

Ah, joy ! The Heart that loves her best
  Is hers — forever hers. The Spouse
  She chooses for her maiden vows
The truest is and worthiest.

And since her hand in thine was given,
  Sweet Mother, whisper to thy Son
  To set the jewel He has won
Luminous in His crown in heaven.
1870.

VEILED [1]

"Dilectus meus mihi, et ego Illi." — Cant. ii. 16.

NO bridegroom mine of change and death:
My orange-flowers shall never fade.
Immortal dews will gem the wreath
When crowns of earth have all decayed.

No bride am I that plights her troth
With touch of doubt, or trust too fond;
And risks the present, wisely loath
To search too far the veil'd beyond.

To me 'tis but the past is veiled —
The world that mocks with joys that fleet;
The " Egypt " that so long has failed
To make its " troubled waters " [2] sweet:

The world with all its sins and cares,
Its sorrows gained and graces lost;
The garden of a thousand snares,
The barren field of blight and frost.

But shines the future clear as truth : —
A few swift years of prayer and peace,

---

[1] Written, at the same lady's request, for the occasion of her taking the veil.   [2] Jer. ii. 18.

Where hearts may know perennial youth,
    And virtues evermore increase:

And then my Lord, my only love,
    Shall come, and lift the veil, and say:
" Arise, all fair, my spouse, my dove!
    The rain is over — haste away!

" The rain is o'er, the winter gone,[1]
    That sun and summer seem'd to thee.
If sweet the toilsome journey done,
    How sweeter now thy rest shall be!"

April, 1871.

TO ST. MATTHIAS

DEAR Saint, thy feast reminds me that to-day,
    Nine years ago, I knelt to Mother Rome,
    To be taken to her bosom — the true home
Found late, yet timely (nor in vain, I pray).
Chosen, perchance (if 'tis not rash to say —
    If ever undeserv'd such graces come) —
    Chosen, like thee, to fill the place of some

[1] Cant. ii. 10, 11.

Ingrate who had thrown his childhood's faith
    away:
Nay, called to share the Apostolic gift
    Of priesthood with thyself: I boldly claim
Thee patron.   Deign be with me when I lift
    My hands to bless, my voice to guide or
    blame:
Nor let the old enemy, who thought to sift [1]
    The Twelve as wheat, bring me to Judas'
    shame.

1875.

IN RETREAT

" BREAK, my heart, and let me die!
    Burst with sorrow, drown with love!"—
Lord, if Thou the boon deny,
    Thou wilt not the wish reprove.

Whence that burning, piercing ray,
    Seem'd to reach me from the light
Where behind the veil 'tis day —
    Where the Blessèd walk in sight?

[1] St. Luke xxii. 31.

Thine, 'twas Thine, O Sacred Heart!
  Mercy-sent, that I might see
Something of the all Thou art,
  Something of the naught in me.

Ah, I saw Thy patient love
  Watching o'er me year on year;
Guarding, guiding, move for move —
  Always faithful, always near!

Saw this self — how weak, how base! —
  Still go sinning, blundering on:
Thankless with its waste of grace,
  Wearied with the little done.

Then I murmur'd: "O my King,
  What are all my acts of will?
Each best effort can but bring
  Failure and confusion still!

"This poor heart, which ought to burn,
  Smoulders feebly; yet may dare
Offer Thine one last return —
  One fond, fierce, atoning prayer?

"Let it break this very hour —
  Burst with sorrow, drown with love!
For if Thou withhold Thy power,
  Thou wilt not the wish reprove." . . .

Past that moment: but, as fall
   Mothers' whispers, answer'd He:
"Daily die [1] — with thy St. Paul:
   Die to self, and live to Me."

LAKE GEORGE, September, 1877.

TURN FOR TURN

JESUS, my King, I have crucified Thee:
   Now it is Thy turn to crucify me.
Make Thou the cross — be it only like Thine:
Mix Thou the gall — so Thy love be the wine.

Shrink not to strip me — of all but Thy grace.
Stretch me out well, till I fit in Thy place.
Here are my hands (felon hands!) and my feet:
Drive home the nails, Lord: the pain shall be
    sweet.

Raise me, and take me not down till I die.
Only let Mary, *my* Mother, stand by.
Last, let the spear while I live do its part: —
Right thro' the heart, my King — right thro' the
    heart!

September, 1878.

[1] I Cor. xv. 31.

PART II

FROM 1878 TO 1897

VOCATION

I

THRICE sacred feast, thrice dear for ever-
more !
The day my Queen ascended to her throne
(Those long, long years of weary waiting o'er),
To reign for *us* — our Mother still, our own :
The day my sister stood beside the Font,
In her eleventh summer, to be born
Of water and the Spirit (she is wont
To keep it as her truer natal morn) :
And now the day when, robed in bridal white,
She plighted troth to Him she would espouse.
And happy I was there to hear her plight
That trustful earnest of the lifelong vows.
Ay, and to win, thro' her fond prayer, a grace
Should draw me with her in the upward race.

II

Thro' her fond prayer. For, passing where she
stood,

In veil and wreath, waiting the bishop's Mass
(So pure she look'd, I scarcely dared intrude
    Upon her thought, yet could not help but
        pass),
I heard my name.   "Dear brother, if so true
    That graces ask'd at our prostration prayer [1]
Are surely granted, tell me what for you?"
    And I: "That our sweet Lady may declare
Her will for me."   For I had needed long
    Such token.   And behold, the answer came—
Came with the morrow!   But a touch, yet strong
    To kindle in my soul a new-born flame—
Like that which burst in sacrificial blaze
From the thick water at the sun's first rays. [2]

NOVICE

O BLESSÈD Crucifix, you teach me this:
    How Jesus' dying love is best repaid.
You bid me daily come and kneel to kiss
    Each Wound my sins have made.

---

[1] The postulant for vestition (*i.e.* each candidate for the habit of religion) prostrates while a solemn litany is said.   And this is believed to be a particularly "acceptable time."

[2] 2 Mach. i, 19–22.

That so my heart may cherish deep within
  A tender memory full of gracious power —
To keep me true, and shame me off from sin,
  And guide me hour by hour.

How shall I dare to kiss those piercèd Feet,
  And wander still, or choose again to stray?
How deem, with fools, perdition's path so
      sweet —
  The broad, smooth, hellward way?

Or how, in sensual sloth or base disgust,
  Turn from that other, which the worldling
      scorns?
Nor bless its very narrowness, and trust
  The hedge of saving thorns?

And those dear Hands — almighty, yet, for me,
  Nail'd helpless there! Shall ever guilty deed
Tempt mine again, and I, consenting, see
  The red gash freshly bleed?

Those Hands so full of merit and of grace,
  Shall mine not haste to gather while they may,
The treasure which will bid me take my place
  Upon His right that day?

And last, the dearest Wound of all, which laid
   The still'd Heart open to the core, to show
That it had burst with very love and paid
   Its uttermost of woe !

Shall I, then, coldly view that open Side,
   Nor take the sheltering home it fain would
      give —
Like the ark's door of mercy, standing wide,
   That all may pass and live ?

Love calls for love.   Ah, where is mine, if He,
   This Prince of lovers, woo me with such pain
To live for Him as He has died for me —
   And sue me but in vain ?

1879.

PROFESSED

O CRUCIFIX, the book of books thy name!
   Thou tellest of a King who left His
     throne
To seek a death of agony and shame
   For love of me — to win me for His own.

His love, the thorns have writ it on His Brow,
   The scourges on His Body — ah, how plain !
Yet seems it I am only learning now
   To read a story conn'd and conn'd again.

A silent wooer, He : His master-art
   A ruddy mouth in Foot or Side or Hand :
Five eloquent Wounds, which utter from His
      Heart
   A voice all hearts were made to understand.

But now from out these Wound-Mouths seems
      to well
   A strange new music, thrilling through and
      through :
As if my soul had never caught the spell
   Of half they say, tho' owning all for true.

Then is it that divinest charm of love —
   That freshness, evermore like morning new —
Which waits to crown our brimming cup above,
   Yet drops us here some foretaste of its dew ?

Or what the cause of this new meaning found
   In tale so old ?   Ah yes, it is, in part,

That nameless charm : but more, that I am
    bound
  In closer ties to each dear Sacred Heart.

" Christo confixus cruci " [1] — nail for nail :
  By three strong vows death-wedded to my
    Lord.
And by the fourth [2] — of faithful tender wail —
  Transfixus,[3] too, with Mary's very sword.

SACRED HEART RETREAT,
    LOUISVILLE, KY.,
       September, 1880.

———◆———

THREE DAYS

I

ENTRANCE

THY faith, St. Hélena, be mine to-day!
  Like thee I come to seek and find the
    Cross :

---

[1] Gal. ii. 19. "I am fastened with Christ to the Cross."

[2] The Passionists take a Fourth Vow — of promoting devotion to the Passion.

[3] "Transpierced." Our Lady's Dolors at the foot of the Cross are called by the Church her "Transfixion."

For me the true one, as I dare believe.
Small care was thine what prudent folk might
   say
   Of toil and treasure spent on likely loss,
      All for a dream — not sent thee to deceive.

Such dream be mine.   A greater Queen than
   thou —
   The Empress-Mother of the Lord of all —
      Bids even me ascend the Mount of Myrrh,
The Hill of Incense,[1] to the very brow!
   Ah, could she let me heed a fancied call,
      When well she knows I climb for love of
      her?

May 3, 1879.

II

VESTITION

" The dream holds true," I murmur'd, quite at
   rest,
   Kneeling a postulant at Vesper choir
      Before our Lady's altar, to be clad,
As our Saint Paul was, in the sable vest

---

1 "I will go unto the mountain of myrrh and to the hill of
incense." — First antiphon at Lauds, Office of Seven Dolors.

Which *she* wore first,[1] and he at her desire —
    Himself a dreamer the wise world calls
        mad.

It was the farewell even-song of May —
    Feast of Our Lady of the Sacred Heart:
        Her choice I knew — too precious to be
           lost.
Ay, and, of course — for me — a Saturday
    (That day of mercies on my life's strange
        chart);
        And Vigil of divinest Pentecost.

And first they clothed me with the garb which
        mourns
    So faithfully our Saviour's rueful death:
        Then on my shoulder the symbolic cross,
And on my head they placed the crown of
        thorns:
    Bidding me take one long prayer-wafting
        breath,
    Then up the steep, to win by happy loss.

May 31, 1879.

---

[1] Our Lady appeared to him wearing the habit.

III

PROFESSION

" The dream holds true," I murmur'd, full of
    peace,
    As prostrate at the altar's foot I lay,
      While one in stole funereal o'er me read
The Passion from Saint John. How sweetly
    cease
    All fears in those who seek but to obey,
      And, deaf to self, ask only to be led !

Then, kneeling with my hands in his who gave
    The habit, I pronounced the holy vows
      Which wed me to Religion — and to this
Stern family, that ever, blithely brave,
    Sings to the Church the wooing of her
      Spouse :
      Recounts the Sweat of Blood, the Traitor's
      Kiss,

The clotted Scourges, the thorn-woven Crown,
    The carried Cross, and all the dolorous
      Way :
      The following Mother, too, with sinless
      Heart

Sword-riven; the three dark hours; the taking
    down;
  The Tomb; and desolation's woe, that lay
    Heaviest of all — for *He* no more had part.

And I have pledged me to join chorus well,
  Hymning this sweeter tale of truer love
    Than ever poet feign'd.   O Mother mine,
Thy bosom be my school!   There let me
    dwell,
  To catch the mystic moanings of the dove —[1]
    Faint-echoed in all other souls from thine.

June 1, 1880.

SONNETS ON THE WAY OF THE CROSS

I

'TIS I have sinn'd, and Thou art doom'd to die:
  Thy death my life! . . . What answer
    shall I make?

---

[1] A principal reason why the Church is called a "dove" in the Canticles is because of her sympathy with the Passion of her Spouse. Our Lady, then, as the type of the Church, is also the "dove," by reason of her Com-Passion, her Dolors.

But this: that what Thou givest I will take —
Take and go free? . . . What life, then, Lord,
 have I
Apart from Thine? What easeful liberty,
 Thou standing here a captive for my sake?
If erst I dreamt of such, now, wide awake,
I find my only freedom *not* to fly.

My King, let me die with Thee — die to all
 I lived for once without Thee. Let me taste
  Thy chalice with Saint John, Thy Passion
  share
With Magdalen. For Thou hast deigned to call
 My fickle soul to gird her loins in haste
  And march with those who boldly, sternly
  dare!

II

The Cross! . . . A slave's death for the King
  of kings! . . .
 Ay, but that King has made Himself a slave:[1]
 Thy slave, my soul — whom He has stoopt to
 save
From feller servitude than clanks and clings

[1] Phil. ii. 7. "Slave" is the accurate rendering of the word in both the Greek text and the Latin.

In convict chains, or tyrannously wrings
  The exile's heart by some Siberian grave:
  A bondage where the joys thou needs must
    crave
Had been as far from hope as angel wings!

Slave of thy love, He takes the Cross: and see
  How tenderly He clasps it — like a spouse!
    Then wilt not thou, in turn, accept, embrace,
Here at His side, the cross He wills for thee?
  No grievous yoke, but one His love *allows* —
    Proof of forgiving, pledge of crowning,
      grace!

III

So weak, my King!   Almighty, yet so weak!
  Then is it that our sins so heavily lay
  On One Who might have smiled them all
    away
And left His justice not a claim to wreak?
Nor rather that, by this surpassing freak
  Of charity, Thy tender Heart would stay
  Our fainting souls and tottering steps, and say
(As Thy Apostle learnt of Thee to speak):

" Is any weak, I not?   Shall any take
  Their cross to follow Me, and fall at the start,

Nor be in *this* like Me? . . . Then, fear
  not blame.
Be but content to suffer for My sake
  Each seeming failure — till thou win thy part
    In that rich glory which has crown'd My
    shame.

IV

His Mother comes to meet Him. O my Queen,
  Will any say thou comest late? Not I.
Since thou didst give Him up to go and die,
All hast thou witnessed, tho' thyself unseen.
Thy Heart has answer'd His with pangs as keen
  For every sting of scourge and thorn and lie,
  The " Ecce Homo ! " and the rabble's cry,
And Pilate washing hands he could not clean.

But now thy Jesus His triumphal way
  Begins, 'tis thine to meet Him with His load,
    And share it soul to soul, O brave and true !
And shall not *we*, in turn, who day by day
  Follow cross-laden, find upon the road,
    As surely waiting, *our* sweet Mother too ?

V

Right scornfully the forced Cyrenian lends
  The timely help we envy as we gaze :

But Jesus blesses him, and Mary prays;
And soon his will, no less than body, bends.
Oh, how his heart now glows, as he befriends
That beauteous Pair the sudden light arrays!
And on he plods, lost in a sweet amaze;
Till — all too short for him — the long march
    ends.

My soul, behold thy perfect model here!
    The cross thou needs must carry, wouldst
        thou live :
    But see, 'tis sharing in a task divine!
Thy Saviour goes before thee; but so near,
    He asks the very aid Himself must give!
        'Tis His Cross thou art bearing — and He
            thine!

VI

That Face!   Ah, who would know it for
    divine —
    The thorn-pierced brow, the furrow'd cheek,
        the eyes
Blood-blinded?
            Only hearts that faith makes wise.
And such, dear Saint Veronica, was thine :
Illumed to see the hidden Godhead shine,

And thus the tender ministry devise
Which earn'd so well the picture's sweet sur-
    prise —
A treasure for the nascent Church to shrine.

Let me too, sister, keep that Face so fair.
    Pray it may haunt me with its pleading woe!
      For when was love so eloquently writ?
But in my soul, my life — reflected there,
    In my fulfill'd vocation — let it show;
      Abiding bright while earthly shadows flit!

VII

A second fall, and heavier!   Pitiless sod,
    How canst thou wound thy Maker?

                        Harder still
    The hearts that love Him not, but set their
      will
Averse, and sullenly spurn their Saviour-God!
Worse than those ruffian hands, with lash and
    rod,
    That strike His prostrate form — and send a
      thrill,
    Perchance, into some bosom, thence to fill
With timely sorrow for a path long trod.

Ah, was it not, dear Lord, beholding these —
  The many who would turn their gaze away
    From Thee and Thy sweet Mother in your
      woe —
That sank Thee to the earth?
                    And from Thy knees
  Thou beggest *us* to toil with Thee, and pray,
  And suffer on — tho' all the world should go.

VIII

Not all are hounding Him to death — of those
  Who seem the rabble. Some, of womankind,
  True to their gentler nature, call to mind
His life of gracious wonders 'mid His foes;
And follow but to weep its thankless close
  To these He turns, as comforted to find
  Such mourners with His Mother, tho' so blind
Their sorrow to their own, their children's, woes.

Yea, " blessèd they who mourn," as He hath
    said :
  Most blessed when their tears with Mary's
    flow
    For Jesus' bitter Passion. But in vain
A shallow grief, which feels not *why* He bled.

In vain our pity, if we shrink to know
>Ourselves, our sins — their guilt, their debt
>>of pain.

IX

And yet again Thou fallest — and so nigh
>The journey's end! Ah, wouldst Thou not
>>atone
>For our faint hearts — so niggard to Thine
>>own —
Who quail at crowning cost, and ofttimes fly
The summit's edge, for all our climbing high?
>I ween 'tis this: and yet not this alone;
>But Thy compassion too for nature's moan
At sin's hard doom — necessity to die.

Thyself wilt die; and, dying, vanquish death:
>But first once more be proven very man
>>By mortal dread. Lest, haply, we forget,
As one by one is bidden yield his breath,
>How in dark fear Thy victory began —
>>The cry, the sweat of blood, on Olivet.

X

The wretches strip Him. Ruthlessly, rude hands
>tear

His garments, stubborn with the gory glue,
From off the scourge-plough'd flesh — which
    bleeds anew,
And quivers rawly to the lambent air.
O " my Beloved, white and ruddy " [1]— fair
    Beyond all fairness — how Thy lovers rue
    To see that virginal Body meet the view
Of brutal hate, the scorn of vulgar stare !

But Thou wilt have it — to avenge the blush
    Of outraged modesty for deeds of shame
        Since Eve's sin bred the sacrilege of vice :
Nor lettest Thy astonish'd angels rush
    To guard and screen Thee with their swords
        of flame —
        For this would bar the second Paradise.

Insatiate mockers !   With the wonted wine,
    And kindly numbing myrrh,[2] they mingle
        gall.[3]

---

[1] Cant. v. 10.   [2] St. Mark xv. 23.

[3] St. Matt. xxvii. 34.   It was customary to give criminals before execution a drink of wine and myrrh : the wine being intended to stimulate their nerves, and the myrrh to diminish the sense of pain.   Reading St. Matthew's account, we should infer that the gall was a cruel substitute for the myrrh : but St. Mark

And I, my King!   The offered cup I call
Love and devotion in return for Thine —
How bitter must it taste when I repine
   At some fresh cross, which harder seems than
     all;
   Or self dares count Thy least of wishes small,
And Thou so thoughtful for the least of mine!

Then, here and now, Lord, as I pray Thee strip
   My foolish soul of each new-woven pride,
     And cut each tie which binds me not to
     Thee;
Mix Thou this draught and press it to my lip: —
   The wine, Thy love; the gall, all joys beside —
   Or woes, so Thou hast tasted them for me.

XI

His butchers stretch Him on the altar-wood —
   This meek, mute Lamb of God.   And He
     obeys

expressly mentions myrrh; so that the mockery lay in mingling
gall with the benignant draught.   Moreover, it is significant that
St. Mark does not say that our Saviour tasted the drink, whereas
St. Matthew does.   This shows that our Lord *tasted* the liquid for
the *gall's* sake, and refused to drink further because He would not
have His sense of suffering lessened.   The prophecy of Psalm lxviii.
22 was fulfilled as to the "vinegar" when Jesus cried "I thirst!"

As sweetly now as erst in infant days,
When the new Mother by the manger stood :
For thro' obedience comes redemption's good.
   Ah, *She* is standing here too : tho' with gaze
   Averse, yet listening as the hammer plays
On each blunt nail that spurts the Precious
    Blood !

O Mother's Heart, I cannot ask to feel
   Those pangs of thine — which only do not
    slay
   Because Omnipotence holds thee to live on !
But there's a music in that ringing steel,
   Which make thou haunt me to my dying
    day —
   And most in death, when other sounds are
    gone !

Is it enough to hear those hammers ring ?
   Enough to know their music ?   Love and
    faith
   Its burden.   " See, He loves thee unto
    death —
And this fierce, lingering death ! " the song they
    sing.

Then faith a loveless, love a faithless, thing,
  Which will not "glory in the Cross,"—as
    saith
The rapt Apostle [1]—scorning the false breath
Of worldling homage with its Cæsar-king!

Yea, and thrice blest—a wisdom not for all—
  Who wed them to the Cross, by triple vow,
    Espousing death in life, lest love should
      fail.
'Tis theirs to echo the deep heart of Paul
  With inmost symphony—as I do now:
    " *Christo confixus cruci* " [2]—nail for nail!

XII

A nameless horror over earth and sky
  Creeps darkly.   Nature shudders, and the sun
  Sickens unclouded—as his course were run
For evermore, and he must gasp and die.
On Calvary's dim summit, holding high
  Their burdens, loom three gibbets: and on
    one

[1] Gal. vi. 14.
[2] Gal. ii. 19, "I am fastened with Christ to the Cross."

Hangs the Man-God — His " Hour" at last
    begun :
The Woman, Co-Redemptress, standing by.

Nor she alone.   The faithful John is there ;
    And Magdalen, abandoned to her woe,
        Kneels with white arms about her true
        Love's cross,
Catching His Blood upon her golden hair.
    Queen-penitent, tho' other tears may flow,
        Who shares like thee the sinless Mother's
        loss !

With big, slow moments three dark hours suc-
    ceed :
    Three ages to those aching hearts and eyes
    That watch their dying God.
                    The jeering cries
Of jubilant hate His silence will not heed :
But lo ! Himself has broken it, to plead
 " Father forgive them !": and the Mother
    sighs
    Her pardoning prayer with His : and mercy
    plies
At awe-thrill'd breasts awaking to their need.

And one, at least, accepts the proffer'd grace
  With comforting quickness: even thou, blest
      Thief!
    Pledge that none need despair, however late.
Yet let presumption fear that other's place,
  Who swells the bitter sea of Mary's grief,
    And dies at Jesus' side — a reprobate!

"Woman, mine hour is not yet come," He said
  At Cana's marriage-feast; beholding there
  His own espousals with the Bride "all fair,"[1]
And what red dower the Mystic Vine must shed
For Eucharistic banquet ere they wed:
    Yet granted the anticipating prayer,
    To show what advocate beyond compare
Should one day stand us in a mother's stead.

But now has come that Hour.   Again He calls
  Her "Woman" — Second Eve.   "Woman,
      behold ·
    Thy son!"   He says — my Church: the
      child no less
Of thy Heart than of Mine.
                              Creative falls

[1] Cant. iv. 7.   Of course, by the "Bride" I mean the Church.

That word.   Henceforth her bosom can enfold
  Us all with true maternal tenderness.

" Behold thy Mother ! "   Words He might have
    said
  At Bethlehem, from the crib ; for she was then
  New Eve, and Mother of our Life : or
    when
He rose, the deathless " first-fruits [1] of the dead " ;
Or forth to Bethany His lov'd ones led [2]
  To watch the heavens receive Him out of ken.
  But no : He chose this Hour : and caused the
    pen
Of him who *heard* to write what we have read.

Yes, dearest Lord !   Our Mother was to be
  By Thy gift doubly ours.   And Thou didst
    wait
    Till she had shared Thy Passion — seen
    Thee prove
Thy love for us, and proved her own for Thee
  To last excess : *then* solemnly instate
    The Queen of mercy in her realm of love.

[1] 1 Cor. xv. 20.
[2] St. Luke xxiv. 50.

" Amen, amen, I say to thee this day
   Shalt thou with me in Paradise repose.". . .
   Poor recompense, this garner'd *one*, for those
Innumerous scorners in malign array
Who forced His sweat of blood!   With fresh
      dismay
   He sees them now; and feels again the
      throes
   Of fruitless travail — keenest of all woes
To love like His, and last to pass away.

May well, then, from His soul's depths burst
      the cry,
   " My God, My God!   Why hast forsaken
      me ? "
      Why left me helpless to my love's
      defeat ?
O mystery of sin — unanswer'd " Why " !
   But 'tis to let Him conquer we are free :
      Must else ourselves that bitter wail repeat.

"I thirst !"   The same wild plaint.   More souls
      to save !
   Ay, more to suffer, could it rescue all ! . . .
   Alas, the vinegar mocks Him like the gall !

" 'Tis finish'd ! " then.   The cup His Father
 gave
Is drain'd save death.   (His Sabbath in the grave
 Awaits Him but as victor of its thrall.)

 Ah ! . . . awful voice ! Is it the judgment-
  call —
That cowering earth shakes like a storm-caught
 wave ? . . .

" Into Thy hands, O Father, I commend
 My spirit ! "   Then the bow'd head yields
  the ghost. . . .
  Eternal God, life's Master, deigns to die !
O mourning universe, well mayst thou rend
 Thy hardest rocks !   But human hearts can
  boast
 A sterner adamant — and still defy !

His death our life.   This many a gaping tomb
 Attests — disgorging its long-moulder'd prey.
 Old Adam's tomb is here, traditions say ;
Beside it Eve's.   I ween earth's second womb
Issues each perfect form.

     And now the gloom
 Lifts softly, and the sun regains his ray :

While evening follows with a calmer sway
Than ever reign'd since Eden ceased to bloom.

Behold the Temple's veil is riven in twain!
  Abides no more the Covenant of Fear. . .
    Hail, law of Love — New Testament of
      grace!
Let the insulting soldier thrust amain!
  Thou touchest the true Door, thou magic
    spear! . . .
    Hail, open'd Heart — our home, our hid-
      ing-place!

XIII

Desolate Mother, sorrow's day has set
  For Him thou claspest there, but not for thee!
  When thou hadst seen thy Jesus' soul go free,
His body was to bear one outrage yet;
And thro' thy own heart went the spear that let
  The mingled stream gush forth.
               And now thy knee
  Supports that Form, all gently from the tree
Down-taken; and, at last, thy lips have met

Each Wound-mouth: how those cruel thorns
    still cling

Among the tangled, ruby-jewell'd gold!
   While the deep lull within thee only wakes
Thy memory the more to each quick sting;
   And woes o'er-past, renewing thus their
      hold,
      Deny the rest *our* worn-out anguish takes!

How readest thou, my Queen, that wondrous
      Book
   Thou bendest o'er, the while with precious
      nard
   Thou closest rift and gash? Dost thou
      regard
Our sins that scored the page? Or rather
      look
At love's sweet argument — His love Who took
   Their penance on Himself, nor deem'd it
      hard?
   Let me not wrong thee. Nothing can retard
Thy pardoning pity. There is not a nook
In all thy bosom, where a moment lurks
   Of aught but love for sinners. Thou didst
      share
      His Passion for their sakes; and didst be-
         come

Their Mother by thy throes.

　　　　　　　　　'Tis this that works
　Within thee — the new mother's tender care
　　That each child-soul shall find thy Heart
　　a home.

XIV

And now the sad procession wends its way
　To Joseph's garden.   As a maiden womb
　First held that Body, so a maiden tomb
Receives it for the birth of Easter-day.
Yes, dearest Mother, let His rich friends lay
　Thy treasure here, amid the vernal bloom,
　Which breathes of life, not death — of joy,
　　not gloom :
Fit rest for One who cannot know decay.

Thine the last touch; the last look thine.

　　　　　　　　　'Tis o'er !
　Thou goest home with John and Magdalen :
　　Two broken hearts; but not so lone as
　　thine,
Tho' strangers to thy peace — and evermore
　Forgetful of the promised morrow, when
　　Their eyes shall greet again that Face
　　divine.

Thyself "a garden enclosed," like that where
    lies
  Thy buried Love : yea, and "a fountain
    seal'd " [1] —
Seal'd like His sepulchre. For unreveal'd
Thy sorrow's depths — ev'n to the angel eyes
That watch thy vigil for the Easter skies,
  And see thy soul a stainless light congeal'd.

Yet mortal sight, by faith's anointing heal'd,
Discerns the Spouse-Church — veil'd in mystic
    guise.

We hail thee, "at the Cross thy station keep-
    ing,"
  Our Priestess at the altar of all time —
    The Church at Mass. So here, in equal
      measure —
Thy whole life centred where thy Lord is sleep-
    ing —
  Thou imagest the Church with trust sublime
    Guarding the Host, her tabernacled treas-
    ure.

          [1] Cant. iv. 12.

TO ST. JOHN

TO-DAY my task is ended; and to-day,
  Virgin Apostle of the Sacred Heart,
Thy octave closes.   Ah, then, deign impart
Thy blessing to these sonnets.   Let me lay
The poor fond tribute I have dared to pay
    At such a shrine, with weak, presuming
    art —
    Yet vow'd to traffic in this holy mart —
In thy chaste hands; and ask thee, if I may,
To offer it to Her whom I too call
My Queen and Mother.
                              She will sweetly take
    The gift from thee, her first adopted son;
And then, in turn, present it — and with all
    Her Heart to Jesus: Who, for *that* love's
    sake,
    Will smile upon it as a thing well done.

OCTAVE OF ST. JOHN THE EVANGELIST,
        Jan. 3, 1882.

EASTER

I

RIGHT peacefully He rests: while vigilant
　　hate
　Seals the great stone — as if, forsooth, to show
　　More gloriously the triumph of its Foe;
And sets its valiant guard — to earn the fate
Of bribing " sleeping witnesses "[1] too late.
　　But is not love awake?　If, kindly slow,
　The Sabbath-hours glide softly o'er the woe
Of hearts too crush'd — save one — to hope and
　　　wait;

That ONE is watching — faithfully — alone:
　A trancèd vigil: even thine, my Queen!
　　And sees thy soul His spirit move in light,
From Abraham's Bosom thro' each dimmer zone
　Of Limbus; till its beauty glads, I ween,
　　Socrates', Plato's, Virgil's,[2] yearning sight.

---

[1] St. Augustine.

[2] Sister Catharine Emmerich saw our Lord descend into the limbus of the Pagans. I have been told also, by a well-informed theologian, that Plato appeared one day to some ancient writer who had been berating him for his errors, and said: " Why are you calling me such hard names?　When our Lord came down into the limbus of the Pagans, I was the first to greet Him, and He spoke

II

The long night wanes.   Dawn's first touch grays
    the East.
At the seal'd sepulchre the watchmen pace
Less sullenly — soon to quit the gloomy place;
And curse the craven fears of Scribe and Priest.
But lo, this instant, while they guess it least,
    The tomb is empty!
                On our Lady's face
A glory falls.   She wakes in the embrace
Of Him Who brings her joy's eternal feast!

O recompense of sorrow!   Whose the lyre
    Shall worthily hymn that ecstasy of rest?
    No strain of mortal bard; nor ev'n the lays
Which wing to God from each Angelic Choir:
    No, nor thy own full heart, O Mother blest!
    But His alone thro' Whom is perfect praise.

III

And now the sun a blood-red shaft has thrown
    O'er doom'd Jerusalem.   When lo, a light

very kindly to me."   In Montalembert's "Monks of the West,"
too, we have the beautiful story of the monk who prayed for Virgil,
and presently heard a soft voice which bade him continue to pray,
that they might one day "sing the mercies of God" together.

Bursts sudden on the guards' astonished sight,
From giant form to heathen creed unknown!
Earth quakes beneath his step: the great seal'd
   stone
Rolls at his touch aside.   So dazzling bright
His face, the soldiers swoon in deadly fright;
Then flee, and leave him calmly throned — alone.

Prince[1] Michael this.   And next, the Princes[2]
   twain,
Gabriel and Raphael, take within the cave
   Their seat, to wait the Magdalen's brave
      quest.[3]
But *she* will hear "Why weepest thou?" in vain:
   And weeping linger by the empty grave,
      Till He is found — her love, her life, her
         rest.

IV

Many and sure the proofs which Jesus gave
   That He had "risen indeed"; but one, to me,
Dearest of all.
            He knew the times to be:
And let His own Apostle doubt, to save

---

[1] Dan. xii. 1.   [2] Ibid. x. 13.
[3] St. John xx. 1, 11, 12, etc.

Our tempted faith.[1]　Ay, knew, too, we should
　　crave,
　From very faith (else where our love ?), to *see*,
　O natural Thomas, and to *touch*, with thee,
That glorious Body, spoiler of the grave.
And ah, He keeps the death-marks of His
　　choice —
　Five shining Wounds — five rosy mouths, to
　　plead
　　With Him for mercy, and with us for love !
How safely we can trust their tender voice !
　Yea, and that Mother who beheld them bleed
　Still reads *us* in them where she reigns above.

v

Bethink thee, thou that enviest these who *saw*
　Our risen King, what after-life they led :
　To self, to earth, to time, how truly dead —
For they had died with Him.　Their only law
" Thy kingdom come ": in thought, word, act,
　　to draw,
　As risen members of a risen Head,
　Their life from His.　Ah, must it not have sped
Full of deep peace and love's delicious awe ?

[1] See St. Gregory's Homily on the Gospel for the Feast of
St. Thomas (December 21) in the Roman Breviary.

But hast not *thou* died with Him? Hast not been
  " Buried with Him by baptism into death "? [1]
    How fareth, then, *thy* risen life? 'Twill
      thrive
As thou shalt " *daily* die " [2] to self and sin.
  " All for the Sacred Heart! " its very breath —
    Their watchword who " in Christ are made
      alive." [3]

———◆———

"THE LAST HOUR" [4]

" ALL for the Sacred Heart " — watchword
    of Faith!
Ah, how we need it in these selfish days —
We who can feel overcreeping earth's ways
Chills from the vale of the shadow of death!

Low is our sun. 'Twill be setting full soon.
  Yet sweet and warm is its lingering light —
  There, on the hills! . . . We can climb to
    that height? . . .
Winsomest hour, too, this late afternoon.

---

[1] Rom. vi. 14.   [2] 1 Cor. xv. 31.
[3] 1 Cor. xv. 22.   [4] 1 St. John ii. 18.

Ay, we *must* climb, would we breathe the pure
    air.
Is it so hard to live nearer to Heaven ?
Harder, methinks, to stay down unforgiven.
On to those sunlit hills ! Jesus is there.

Mary is calling us.   Hark to Her song :
   " All for the Sacred Heart " — watchword of
    Hope !
Joseph is near us, to help with the slope.
What shall we fear, but to tarry too long ?

Yea, " 'tis the last hour." The sun of our Faith
   Sets on a world that wills darkness for light.
   Souls that would live must ascend to a height
Safe from the chills of the shadow of death.

    VALPARAISO, CHILE,
Feast of the Sacred Heart, 1888.

"RUNNING WATERS"[1]

I KNOW five rivers, flowing night and day
   With swift and voiceful tide :
Yet seen by faith ; and only hearts that pray
   Can hear them as they glide.

  [1] "Cast thy bread upon the running waters." — Eccles. xi. 1.

Rivers of souls.   The first, of all that go
　　Each hour to that wide sea —
Of boundless happiness or shoreless woe —
　　We call Eternity.

And second, the poor souls in mortal sin :
　　But ah, how vast a stream !
Its turbid waters rushing with a din
　　Might wake the worldling's dream !

The narrow third — of all in God's dear grace —
　　Runs purely, brightly, on :
But oft, thro' rocks and bars that break its race,
　　Finds passage hardly won.

Full darkly the broad fourth.   All souls without
　　Their one true home, the Church.
Jews, heathens, Turks : souls groping in their
　　　doubt,
　　Or keen in earnest search :

Some in their errors proudly self-contained ;
　　Some holding quite aloof
In coldest apathy ; some, too, who have gained,
　　Yet spurn, the clearest proof.

Last, the fifth river: murmuring evermore
   The sweet-sad plaint of those
Who, roll'd on fiery billows toward the shore,
   Pine for its blest repose.

     *   *   *   *   *   *

What shall *we* do, then, who have hearts that
     pray ?
   There is a Heart which gave,
Thro' Five glad Wounds, Its life-blood all away
   For every living wave

Of these five streams.   Then, daily let us take
   Drops of that Blood, and shed
Them freely o'er the waters.   Each will make
   Some passing ripple red.

———◆———

MATER DOLOROSA

O MY Queen, we find Thee fairest in Thy
     mortal days of moan :
In the garment of Thy Dolors most our Mother,
     most our own !

Link'd with Thine, our pain and sorrow gain
     a beauty and a worth,

Which, to faith's eye, make them precious —
　　more than any joys of earth :

Treasures we may bring to Jesus, rescued from
　　life's waste and loss —
Offer'd on Thy Heart's pure altar, as Thou
　　standest by the Cross.

———◆———

SEPTEMBER

THE month, my Queen, which brings thy
　　natal day :
　　And yet we give it to thy Dolors Seven !
　　And lo, the strains have scarcely died away
　　　Which hymn'd thy bright Assumption into
　　　　heaven !

But ah, though sinless, thou wast born for woe :
　　For deepest grief no less than highest joy !
　　And since God fashion'd woman's heart, we
　　　know,
　　　Stronger than man's — more pure from self's
　　　　alloy —

He gave to thine a love beyond all love;
    And, with it, strength for pain beyond all
        pain:
That when thy destin'd Spouse, th' Almighty
    Dove,
    From thee, His own "seal'd fountain," free
        of stain,

Should form for us our Jesus' Sacred Heart,
    That Heart might prove the duplicate of
        thine:
Thy love, *thy* sorrow, for its chosen part;
    And only more intense because divine.

What marvel, then, that we, who sing this
    moon
The Triumph of the Cross, beside it place
Thy Seven Swords of woe—and this so soon
    After our gaze upon thine infant face?

Born to be *our* sweet Mother, we remember
    How dear it cost thee. Lovingly we see
The mystic *septem*[1] in the year's September:
    For truly children of thy Dolors we.

[1] Seven. September was the *seventh* month in the old Roman calendar.

AD MARIAM PRO MARIA

I

MOTHER of Sorrows we still call thee, though
   In Paradise thou reignest, tasting naught
   But perfect joy.   More comfort to our thought
Thy mortal sympathy with pain and woe.
Mother of Sorrows, it is mine to know
   One named from thee, of life so trial-fraught,
   Full sure am I of gracious purpose, wrought
For some rare fruit the destined hour will show.

But ah! she needs thy tender help — the might
   Of thy true Heart to lean upon.   I trust
      My sister to thy keeping.   If she share
Thy desolation when the shades of night
   Came down o'er silent Calvary, 'tis just
      She find thy bosom her one refuge there.

II

Keep her in thy Heart for Jesus, sweet my
      Mother, dear my love!
In thine inmost bosom cherish, safe for Him, this
      stricken dove.
She, thy child, her soul would offer victim for a
   work like thine —

Sorrow's victim, grace-united with the Holocaust
   Divine:
Yea, her body too is yielded gladly to the pain
   she braves:
All to save an erring husband — win him to the
   faith that saves.

O that faith! How fair is sorrow Passion-color'd
   by its light!
Beauteous as the dawn of Easter when it broke
   thy vigil's night.
And how merit-strong affliction, wedded to thy
   dying Son!
Every pang a plea availing, every woe a triumph
   won.
Such was thy faith: such my sister's. Keep,
   then, keep this stricken dove
In thine own inviolate bosom, dear my Mother,
   sweet my love!

———◆———

TO MONICA [1]

I THOUGHT to place you in the desolate
   Heart

[1] The "Maria" prayed for above. She has both names.

Of Mary — when she held to it her Dead.
" Yes, dearest Mother, keep her *there*," I said:
" And make her very soul of thine a part ! "

O fond forgetting !   For, in sooth, 'twas there
   I found you — there, at foot of the Cross, we
      met.
   Reminded now, how came I to forget ?
Still, not in vain the oft and tender prayer,

"Sweet Mother, *keep* her there ! " But now I say:
   " And me too with her, in the dolorous core
   Of thy pierced bosom, till I learn a lore
Less hard now such a sister leads the way —

" The lore which maketh saints — the *love* of all
   That self most shrinks from."   Yea, for this
      we met.
   A lesson may I nevermore forget,
Whatever hope recede or darkness fall !

———◆———

TO MARGARET

YOU ask me for a poem, gentle maiden:
   Then be yourself my theme.

In those blue eyes —
Twin lakes inviting summer skies —
I read a soul with sacred sorrow laden;
Yet sunshined with a gleam
Of hope that is no dream.

A dream, were faith a dream and earth its ending:
But never a dream, so long
As God's dear grace
Leaves evil chance no lurking-place;
O'erruling, and to one sweet purpose blending,
Life's joys and sorrows — strong
To right each passing wrong.

What to a heathen mind were ill-starr'd meet-
ing —
A freak of cruel fate —
Has proofs for *you*
Of hidden good, as clear and true
As had you learnt them from an angel's greeting!
And if the light bids wait,
God's time is never late.

A Father's Hand till now has wisely guided:
Not His to lead astray.
O'er all the past —

And most, when seem'd it overcast —
A Mother's heart has tenderly presided.
　　That Hand, that Heart we pray
　　To shape your future way.

And what if peace await you in the treasure
　　Of high vocation stored;
　　　And wonted price
　　Demand — of costly sacrifice?
Who, looking on the Crucifix, dares measure
　　Love to that dying Lord,
　　Like gold from miser's hoard?

Or shall we contemplate the sinless Mother
　　Her post so staunchly keeping
　　　At Jesus' Cross,
　　Nor see the gain of generous loss?
O privileged hearts — their joy beyond all other —
　　Who sow with Mary weeping,[1]
　　To share her Easter reaping!

FEAST OF ST. BARTHOLOMEW,
　　Aug. 24, 1882.

[1] Ps. cxxv. 6.

SOUTHWARD

I

FROM round to round of bluest sea,
    While softest breezes fan the deck,
    I pass serene; and little reck
Of what the morrow's skies shall be.

I pass content, tho', day by day,
    Two shores belov'd — a double home —
    Are left o'er ruthless leagues of foam;
And farther, farther drift away

The forms more dear than any land —
    The beating hearts that love me well,
    And mourn with me the broken spell
Of look, and word, and hand in hand.

I pass content, for this I know:
    The will I follow is not mine,
    But one that speaks with voice divine,
And calmly, wisely, bids me go.

II

And if, in priesthood's middle years,
    I quit old fields, familiar long,

For new and strange — which seems a wrong
To those who chide me thro' their tears :

" Are we, then, such a fruitless toil ? "
   " Who wants you more than we who
      know ? "
   'Tis only that I needs must sow
Where the great Master turns the soil.

And if again my native isle
   I leave afar, with kith and kin,
   Tho' new hope whispers, " Stay, and win
These to the faith " — and sweet her smile :

I yield them to a better care
   Than mine ; and place a proven trust,
   Which cannot crumble into dust
While breathes on high that Mother's prayer.

S.S. PLEIADES, January, 1884.

TO A WIDOWED MOTHER

ON THE DEATH OF HER ONLY DAUGHTER, AGED SEVEN

I

I MOURN with you — but not your child :
　I weep with you — but not for her.
　　How should I grieve that one so blest
　　Has enter'd her eternal rest ?
That one so sweet, so undefiled,
　Shall never walk with feet that err ?

But you — weep on.　A mother's tears
　Are sacred ever, nor can wrong
　　The holiest dead.　And well I know,
　　Dear friend, how keen your bosom's woe.
The sunshine of your widow'd years,
　You fondly hoped would cheer them long,

Has vanish'd.　Ay, 'tis saddest loss !
　But God will make it greater gain.
　　His grace was with you when you knew
　　That she must go, yet, staunchly true
To duty, took the proffer'd cross ;
　Then knelt beside the bed of pain

No longer to avert death's stroke
  But rather woo its kind release.
    "O dearest Mother, ere I tell
    This decade, let my darling dwell
In Heav'n with thee!" . . . 'Twas heard. She
      woke
  To meet God's smile of perfect peace.

II

An earnest of that peace was yours,
  Brave mother, as you bow'd and said
    " My God, I give Thee back my child!"
    Ah, surely, then on *you* He smiled,
And blest with purpose that endures
  Your upward yearning, sorrow-led,

For nobler life.   More grace and more
  Awaits, the promised crown to gem.
    What purifies like loving sorrow
    For faith's to-day and hope's to-morrow?
'Twas Calvary brought our Queen a store
  Of richer joy than Bethlehem.

Of richer joy.   For Her true Heart,
  Thro' all its Dolors' wave on wave,
    Still sang " Magnificat!" and still

Rejoiced in God's exacting will;
Deserving thus Her royal part
In Easter's triumph o'er the grave.

And you, dear friend, ev'n here may know
A foretaste of the bliss to come:
Hold commune with your child, and prove
A tender, ever-watchful love,
Which will not fail, but daily grow —
So *you* draw daily nearer Home.

BUENOS AYRES,
Feast of St. James the Greater,
1885.

———◆———

TO A. W.

I

GO, happy friend: inhale once more
An English summer's balmy breath.
Queen May will welcome you ashore,
And give you purest wine to drink —
The sense of Home: — so sweet, you'll
think
Of Heaven's bright welcome after death.

Ah, *there* our Patria — there is Home —
　　That Heaven! We can but *journey* here
　　　　(In moments when the heart is lonely
　　　　How keenly felt this " exile only " !)
However little we may roam
　　From native land and all that's dear.

In lonelier moments: ay, as when
　　I stood but yester-afternoon
To see you go: and once again,
　　What time I hail'd the soaring moon
That lit so well your Northward prow:
And still — as I am musing now.

II

" Forgive me, Lord," I said to-day,
　　" That I have dared look o'er the sea
　　　　Too fondly tow'rd my own dear land;
And long'd for ev'n a passing stay
　　With those whom I have left for Thee —
　　　　With sister's kiss and brother's hand:

" For here my place — to live or die.
　　Thy work be done: Thy will be mine!"
　　　　And then I thought how *you* will think

Of one who forms a golden link
'Twixt you and years of Southern sky;
   Reminded, as you near the Line,

How he, on deck one April night,
First saw the Great Bear heave in sight,
   Then turn'd to where the Cross still shone;
And all that it had meant for him —
   And still might mean, tho' *that* was gone —
Came o'er him till his eyes were dim :

And sharp the struggle, wild the prayer:
   " Not back to exile !   I am free.
     So Thou but will it.   Let me go
To *my* America — for Thee !
     A larger field to plough and sow,
A richer soil, await me there."

Then came the answer from within —
   The still, small voice, so wondrous strong:
     " Not vainly points yon starry Cross
The only beacon, wouldst thou win
     Eternal gain by present loss;
And shortest route, tho' seeming long."

And so, dear friend, till night is o'er,
  The Cross *your* only light shall be :
      What tho' you find an earthly goal
      In some sweet haven of the soul
  Where circles the " inviolate sea "
The freedom of our England's shore.[1]

BUENOS AYRES,
April, 1885.

------◆------

WHY GOD LOVES US

MY sister said to me one day :
  " You talk of riddles now and then,
  Where simple faith suffices me.
But here's a point beyond my ken,
  Which your philosophy may see :
How God can love us ?   Tell me, pray."

" You wonder how He finds us fair —
  Is that your trouble ? " answer'd I.
    " Yes, that and more.   How He can *love*
  Such nothings to His all ; and why,
    When we offend Him so, and prove
So unresponsive, He can care

[1] The lady has since become a Sister of Mercy in England.

" To sue us with His grace, as tho'
   He needed us," quoth she.   And here
      Her eyes were filling from her heart.
   " It *is* a mystery deep and dear,
      That you would fathom.   Yet, in part,"
I said, " 'tis granted us to know.

" God loves — in all that He has made —
   Himself.   *His* beauty, wisdom, power,
      Shine in His works, or great or small:
In sun and planet, bird and flower.
      Must He not prize, then, more than all,
This soul of ours, whereon is laid

" His very image, like a seal ?
   And if He ' sues us with His grace
      As tho' He needed us,' 'tis plain
   That, thankless as we are and base,
      His glory reaps the larger gain
From working out our perfect weal.

" So, let it pass fond reason's powers,
   How God can wisely love and well
      Such nothings : still, sweet sister mine,
   Our spirits may serenely dwell
      On one sure truth : — that love divine
Loves for its own sake — not for ours."

A BIRTHDAY GREETING

TO S. M. B.

PERHAPS, dear friend, you murmur'd, as
        you woke,
    " Another year of weary, lonely life
    Begins ! Is this the last ? "   And keen the
        strife
For resignation under time's fresh stroke.
But no : I hope a blither spirit spoke
    Within you; pointing upward to a height
    That needs but a little patient climbing —
        quite
Accessible : while easier seem'd the yoke,
Lighter the burden, which the unseen Love,
    Yet scarce believ'd, has laid on you. O trust
        That love ! But suffer with closed eyes its
        sway :
    And soon, true heart, the inexorable *must*
    Will vanish in the privilege of *may*,
As on you journey to your crown above.

Feb. 28, 1878.

TO TERESA LUCY

ON HER BIRTHDAY

I CALL'D you " Tessie with the earnest
    eyes ";
  And when, to-day, I see an image fair
  That comes and goes like some remember'd air
Of sacred music, thus my thought replies :
" May God's dear grace preserve her calm and
    wise
  Like those whose radiant names 'tis hers to
    share —
  Who made the Heavenward path their only
    care,
Yet look'd not fondly for unclouded skies."

Full happy years I wish you ; but implore
  The Saint whose truer natal feast we keep,
    That he, crown'd lover of the " precious
    Cross," [1]
Your master prove in that sublimest lore
  Which lifts the soul from all that worldlings
    weep
  And turns to gold the very dust of loss.

FEAST OF ST. ANDREW THE APOSTLE,
    NOV. 30.

[1] " Salve Crux pretiosa ! " etc. — Antiphon.

TO LUCY TERESA

ON HER TWENTY-FIRST BIRTHDAY

I

LUCY — 'tis a name of light,
  Softly, virginally bright;
Shining from a martyr's brow
  Down the ages like a star;
  With a glory wide and far,
Yet as freshly risen now.

Wear it, then, dear daughter mine,
  As a token grace has given —
Of a call to live for Heaven,
Witnessing [1] to Truth Divine:
Praying still " Thy Kingdom come ! "
  In an age that will not pray —
    In an age that turns from light
    Back to worse than pagan night,
Making life a martyrdom
  Would we " walk as in the day."

With your Saint a martyr *live :*
  Show like her the perfect good
Only Christian faith can give —
  Purest, noblest womanhood.

[1] " Martyr " means " witness."

II

Yes; for you have passed to-day
  Into womanhood's domain.
Girlhood now must drift away
    After childhood's sunny hours :
    Wait you now, for woman's powers,
Deeper joy and higher pain.

Ah, but fear not lest you meet
More of bitter than of sweet !
Crosses to your lot must fall,
  And, it may be, weigh you down ;
But the heaviest of them all
  Surest makes the promised crown.

Lean on Jesus' Heart and Mary's :
Theirs a love that never varies —
Such a tender, patient love,
Brooding o'er us from above,
And in ways not understood
Shaping all things into good.

Let the holy Angels guide you,
  This their month: and one, you know,
Tarries evermore beside you,
  Faithful friend in weal and woe.

Then, too, she whose hallow'd name
Decks your birthday with its fame
(And — devotion wisely shown —
Dear Teresa, 'tis your own);
She will join Saint Lucy's care:
Ay, and something more than share —
Feeding you from volumed store
With a wealth of golden lore.

Hear her speak, while yet she press'd
Onward, upward, to her rest: —
" Suffer naught to mar your peace:
    Tremble not at new or strange:
All things earthly pass and cease:
    God alone will never change!"

FEAST OF ST. TERESA,
    Oct. 15th.

———◆———

SURSUM CORDA

I

I SAW her standing by his grave,
    The grave of him to whom she owes,
    Under God's grace, the faith that glows
Within her bosom pure and brave.

Four years had follow'd on his loss :
   Yet there in summer womanhood,
   Alone, and sweetly constant, stood
The virgin wedded to the cross.

But naught of sadness clouds her life.
   'Tis full of brightness ; rich in power
   To comfort — and with larger dower
Than had she prov'd a happy wife.

Her faith begets an equal hope :
   A hope that sends its music forth
   Like that sweet singer of the North [1]
Who warbles " on the sunrise slope."

II

Not " better to have lov'd and lost
   Than never to have lov'd at all,"
   If death could hold eternal thrall
And mock us with a vanish'd ghost.

But now that we may love and *gain* —
   May hold for aye, in death's despite
   (For this faith gives us with its light) —
Our hearts need never love in vain.

[1] Miss Katherine E. Conway, of Boston, author of " On the Sunrise Slope " and other graceful poems.

When human love leads up to God —
    As yours has led, O true and strong ! —
    Let parting come : 'tis not for long.
The mortal moulders in the sod ;

But, soul with soul communing still,
    Each sunrise nearer brings the morn
    When rosy bliss without a thorn
Shall crown our trust on Sion's hill.

May, 1894.

———————◆———————

TO MOTHER MARY XAVIER THERESA

ON HER GOLDEN JUBILEE [1]

I

'TWAS a jubilee day, our First Mother's
    First Daughter,
When, setting your face tow'rd the Western
    afar,

---

[1] Written for an address from the Sisters of Mercy, at Manchester, N. H.   Mother Ward was Mother McAuley's first professed novice : and she volunteered, with six companions, to come out to the United States at the request of the bishop of Pittsburgh, Pa.

You braved the long leagues of the storm-
    haunted water,
  To follow the shining of Mary the Star.

On toil'd the good ship, bringing nearer each
    morrow
  Its message of mercy, its burden of love:
Seven offerings of faith from the " Island of
    Sorrow " —
  A mystical band with the seal of the Dove.

But you were the chief of that virginal Seven:
  And lo, when their feet touch'd America's
    shore,
'Twas the day your Saint Xavier had landed in
    Heaven!
  And the blessing he gave you abides ever-
    more.

II

Again 'tis a Jubilee Day, dearest Mother!
  Your daughters stand up in this home of the
    free,
And bid to-day echo the joy of another,
  Which dawn'd ere you follow'd the Star of
    the sea.

'Twas the morn of your bridal. The troth
　　you then plighted
How faithfully kept, we your children attest.
You may count us by scores: and we greet
　　you, united
　　With happier scores who have gone to
　　their rest.

This Jubilee Spousal — this calm Golden
　　Wedding —
　　Lights up like a sunset the grace-fruited
　　past:
And we hail in the peace its sweet radiance
　　is shedding
　　A pledge of the glory shall crown you at last.

1882.

———◆———

TO ERIN

I

THE Passion Flower of nations, thou,
　　O Erin, Isle of Sorrow!
Yet ever shines about thy brow
　　The light of Faith's to-morrow.

Where'er thine exiled children go,
   Heav'n smiles benignly o'er them ;
Where'er they turn, in weal, in woe,
   The Cross leads on before them.

O " Populus Apostolus "
   (As Rome's great Council call'd thee) !
'Tis God's high purpose guides thee thus,
   His will that hath enthrall'd thee.

II

When Jesus died, His face was turn'd
   From Salem's thankless city ;
While toward the West his bosom yearn'd
   With love's forgiving pity.

From age to age before Him spread
   The future's wondrous story ;
His eyes each people's annals read —
   Its more of shame than glory.

His Church would conquer far and wide,
   Yet oft the while defeated ;
The scornful robber at His side
   Again, again repeated.

III

He saw *His* Rome, from Satan reft,
   Her empire stronger, vaster,
Than arms and cunning skill had weft
   For earth's now vanquish'd master.

He saw new kingdoms rise and fall,
   Republics thrive and perish . . .
But one dear spot from out them all
   A fonder love should cherish.

A land by rough seas virgin-isled
   I' th' North's half-mythic regions;
Nor, like her sister shore, defiled
   By tramp of Cæsar's legions.

IV

He call'd attendant angels three,
   And sent them swiftly winging
O'er mount and vale and pleasant lea
   Where April green was springing.

" Go, sow my Blood for after years —
   Seven drops of ruby treasure;
And gather from my Mother's tears
   Of pearls an equal measure.

" Go, shed them o'er yon chosen soil :
  The Isle of Martyrs make it.
My grace shall there find richest spoil;
  My mercy ne'er forsake it ! "

IN HONOR OF A GOLDEN WEDDING

A GOLDEN jubilee of wedded life !
    O venerable pair, your plighted troth
  Hath borne the fruits (alas, too rare a growth !)
Of charity and prayer and peaceful strife.
A faithful husband, a devoted wife,
  Look back through fifty summers, and can
      say :
  " Ay, God did surely grant our marriage-day
A blessing with unwonted favors rife.
Of children nine, all live.   And daughters
      twain
  Are vow'd to God in dear St. Joseph's band :
No loss to mourn, but only priceless gain.
While — prouder honor still — 'twas not in vain
  We ask'd that one among our sons might
      stand
  Before God's altar with anointed hand."

HAUD FRUSTRA [1]

" MY King, how barren looks a life-long toil
          In Thy vast field of souls! No sheaf
     appears —
For all Thy promise that who sow in tears
Shall reap in joy! By far the larger spoil
Is claim'd by those Thou settest us to foil —
     Who taunt us with what seem but wasted
          years!
     Ah, make we our account with many fears,
Poor stewards of Thy corn and wine and oil!" [2]

" Use well My grace to do thy little best.
     Not thine to answer further. Leave to Me
          Our seeming failure in the strife with sin.
Some glorify My mercy, and the rest
     My justice. Work in peace. Enough for
          thee
          To know that My elect are gather'd in."

[1] "Not in vain."
[2] "A fructu frumenti, vini, et olei sui: multiplicati sunt."
— Ps. iv., Office of Compline.

A THOUGHT FOR OCTOBER

GOD'S own elect — we know not who they be;
  Yet hour by hour He sees them gather'd in :
Nor all from ways of peace and purity ;
  But more from devious paths, and some from
    haunts of sin.

" From the four winds " His angels gather them :
  And if the many out of favor'd lands,
That hail in Rome the New Jerusalem,
  And touch, for gifts of Heaven, her priests'
    anointed hands ;

Yet not a few from homes of broken truth,
  Where Mother Church an alien must abide ;
And some from darken'd realms in very sooth,
  O'er which the Prince of Hell still lords it
    far and wide.

O Precious Blood, Thou wast not shed in vain
  For these the number'd chosen ones.   But *we*
Must help Thy cause — with prayer and toil
    and pain, —
  And all the more that here we know not
    who they be.

Sweet Angels, teach us to be strong like you
  In patient waiting.   This the month we give
To your dear honor: skies of cloudless blue,
    That speak of Heav'n, and airs that make it
      joy to live.

Ah, pray that while we value things of earth
  As symbol'd well in autumn's rich decay,
Our hearts may wisely treasure at its worth
    Each act for love of souls, done, suffer'd, day
      by day!

———◆———

A THOUGHT FOR NOVEMBER[1]

I

O HOLY Souls, for whom we pray,
  Abide ye near, or far away?
At times we think you very far;
As when we watch the evening star,
And muse if some be prison'd there —
If penal world can shine so fair:
Or when, on some still, tender night,
  The very moonlight seems a wrong —
Shed from an orb of wreck and blight,

[1] First published in *The Poor Souls' Advocate.*

Where moaning ghosts must wander long
O'er barren plain and airless height,
Beneath extremes of fiercer hold
Than tropic heat or polar cold.

II

Yet well I ween ye never leave
  This planet till the blissful hour
When, durance o'er, ye cease to grieve
  And pass to realms of kingly power.
But some beneath earth's surface keep
  Their darksome vigil; others roam
The desert sands, the wind-swept deep;
  And some, more favor'd, haunt the home
Their childhood loved, or where they died.
Yet all are purged and purified
  By pains intense we cannot guess —
    Or searching, sacramental fire,
      Or darkness to which night were day:
  What tho' they be at peace no less,
    And gladly suffer while they pray —
     Their thought of thoughts, their one desire,
    To *see* the God in whom they live,
The Infinite Beauty, and possess
    That All His Face alone can give.

THE LAW OF LIBERTY[1]

I

A^H me, how very guileless once was I!
　　As good a child as ever said its prayers
In blissful ignorance of by and by,
　　Or prattled of its joys and wept its cares
　　As though they were the great world's chief
　　　affairs.
How black was then the whitest shade of wrong!
　　How base to fly a footstep on the stairs!
Ah, that first sense of guilt, so keen and strong —
That instinct for God's rights — we strangle it
　　ere long!

And wherefore?　To be *free:* free to enjoy —
　　To follow our own bent.　At first in things
Of little harm and natural to a boy:
　　But soon — it may be ere a dozen springs
　　Have bloom'd the bower of innocence — there
　　　sings
A bird that lures us with its magic lay,
　　Or merely with the glitter of its wings,
To chase it: and we ramble — on — away —
Heedless of any voice that warns us not to stray.

---

[1] St. James i. 25.

Or if not far we wander, but return
　　While yet 'tis May, the virgin bower is gone.
And oh, how seldom from our loss we learn
　　A knowledge that would make us kings, if
　　　　won,
　　And wiser than the sated Solomon !
Far easier 'tis to wander soon again,
　　And then more wildly, daringly, run on,
All reckless of return — however plain
Th' inevitable end, foreshown us pain by pain.

II

God and His rights grown irksome to our will,
　　The rebel flesh bids intellect arise —
Hurl doubts at faith — defy the threaten'd ill —
　　Mock at the preacher — catch the gay replies
　　Of older fools, and flaunt them in the eyes
Of younger.　And, if fires Lucretian glow
　　Within us, " Alma Venus " takes the skies,
Sole deity : " Fœda Superstitio " [1]
Gulfing the rest, with all the nightmare realm
　　　　below.

---

[1] See the opening lines of Lucretius' great poem, " De Natura
Rerum."

Thus burst our youthful fetters, are we free?
  Have brain and heart the scope which man-
    hood craves?
Ay, free, forsooth, if so the ship at sea
  Sans chart or compass, scorning winds and
    waves!
Right gallantly our self-steer'd vessel braves
A fogg'd horizon, or "an isle misdeem'd";
  But finds no shore—unless where lower slaves
Than Circe's own (for *there* the beast but *seem'd*) [1]
Invite us to despair of all we have fondly dream'd.

And well for some if they but make that strand,
  And taste the cup Circæan. One I know
Who deigns ev'n there to reach a rescue's hand,
  Which some have touch'd, as Mercy's annals
    show.
But sullen pride, its own relentless foe,
Drives on forever, like the Phantom Bark,
  Let tempest lash or gentlest breezes blow.
In vain the Sea Star beacons through the dark:
In vain the red Cross gleams from Peter's saving
    Ark!

---

[1] The enchantress gave her guests a drink which turned them
into beasts. — Homer's "Odyssey."

III

Poor youth! If pitying manhood would but
    draw
This lesson from thy follies, it were well : —
For Freedom Order lives ; for Order, Law —
    The Law which sanctions everlasting Hell.
    Thus Satan learnt, and those that with him
        fell ;
And Adam, when he pluck'd the fatal tree.
    Too late for the lost angels, doom'd to dwell
In hopeless exile : and for us, if we
" Abide not in the Truth "[1]— the Truth which
    " maketh free."

" What is the Truth ? " Who ask with Pilate,
    find
No answer : for they *seek* not while they ask ;
But either smile with will-averted mind,
    Or shirk the burden of an earnest task.
    Ne'er wore humility the sceptic's mask,
Nor " honest doubt "[2] play'd trifler. Say thy say,

[1] Our Lord says of Satan that he "abode not in the truth."
[2] Tennyson's phrase :
    " There lives more faith in honest doubt,
        Believe me, than in half the creeds."

Agnostic !   'Tis thy pride, that loves to bask
In passing sunshine of a frivolous day —
'Tis pride's, not reason's, voice — that boasts it
 cannot pray.

To call " Unknowable " the Greek's " Un-
 known "
Is turning back to worse than pagan night.
The Athenian's altar made a stepping-stone,
 To reach up tow'rd a Father " out of sight."
 He blush'd not to *adore* the Perfect Right,
The Beautiful and Good, of Plato's thought
 And Aristotle's logic : reason's light
Bearing him witness that itself is caught
From an Eternal Mind, as sage and poet
 taught.

IV

What is the Truth ?   The order God has will'd
 Whereby the creature shall its end attain.
For this came down of old the Word that thrill'd
 The patriarchal bosom, nor in vain
 To Moses and the Prophets spake again :
The Word that promised a Redeemer's birth,
 And told how God Himself would not disdain

To stand Incarnate on our sinful earth
And make Obedience shine a thing of matchless
    worth.

By disobedience fell the blight of sin
    On this fair world: and through the woman
      first.
'Twas fitting, then, redemption should begin
    With woman, and be thus our loss reversed.
    To Mary, Second Eve, no spirit accurst,
But Heaven's bright angel, enter'd where she
      pray'd;
    Revealing to her heart, for God athirst,
The love Divine that will'd her Mother-Maid:
And her humility's gladness peacefully obey'd.

Then Jesus, Second Adam, born to do
    His Father's will in all things, not His own,
Did set such pattern of obedience true,
    From Bethlehem's cave to Calvary's dying
      moan —
    Ay, even to the seal'd sepulchral stone —
That, first and last, a holocaust was He.
    And now — though seated on His glory's
      throne:

For still He deigns our Sacrifice to be —
In Eucharistic life obeying men like me !

v

I ween, then, 'tis Obedience holds the key
    Of Wisdom's temple.   " You shall know the
        Truth,"
Said Jesus ; " and the Truth shall make you
        free."
    Yet 'tis a bondage too, in very sooth —
    This freedom : spurn'd by folly-blinded youth,
But welcom'd as the Master's " easy yoke,"
    When God's dear grace infuses timely ruth,
Nor deals His justice we have dared provoke
(A payment long o'erdue) the swift avenging
        stroke.

Light yoke of Christ, that sets His bondsmen
        free
    From lust of selfish heart and lawless brain !
" Come, all ye weary ones, and learn of Me.
    Cease chasing shadows — taking loss for gain.
    My Church shall make the Homeward journey
        plain ;
Her voice Mine own, as all who heed it know :

Shall heal and nourish, comfort and sustain,
With aids it cost My Passion to bestow.
Believe, obey, and find Heaven's foretaste here
  below."

With mind like ours, and tender human heart,
  'Tis thus He draws us to the perfect good :
Knowing we cannot live from Him apart,
  And all our needs divinely understood.
  Nor can we doubt His sweetness, if we would :
Since, while demanding of our love His due,
  He shares the claim with Mary's Motherhood;
And bids us wear *Her* bonds about us too,
And own Her Queen indeed — of beauty pure
  and true.

———◆———

GOD LOVED IN NATURE

TO own, my God, Thy wisdom and Thy
  power,
  As seen in Nature with her deeds and laws,
  Is reason's homage to the Primal Cause.
Thy beauty, too, in star and bird and flower,
In tint and hue, in Spring's aye-virgin dower,

In all things fair, would woo the heart to love,
  Tho' known not that "in Thee we live and
    move " —
Thy Presence all about us every hour.

But we, whose light is Thy Redeemer-Word,
  Whose reason Thou hast glorified with faith,
We call Thee not alone Creator-Lord,
  But Father, Saviour, Lover, in one breath :
And *our* hearts, when Thy wondrous works we
    see,
Exhale the Passion Flower of Charity.

———◆———

A THOUGHT FOR TRINITY SUNDAY

IS music but the poetry of sound —
  Melodious noise, tumultuous harmony ?
An art, a science, with its birthplace found
  In Jubal, son of Lamech's minstrelsy ? [1]
Nay, music is a language born in Heaven ;
  Nor then create, but of eternal birth :
Ere stood before the Throne the Spirits Seven,

[1] Gen. iv. 21.

Or quiring angels hymn'd the nascent earth.
God's utter'd Word; the evermore begetting
   Of the Co-Equal, Co-Eternal Son:
Their mutual Love — that tide forever setting
   Back to its source: the perfect Three-In-
      One: —
Lo, here the primal music! Hence were drawn
Law, Order, Beauty, with Creation's dawn.

———◆———

TO NATURE

NATURE, to me thy face has ever been
   Familiar as a mother's; yet it grows
   But younger with the wearing years, and
     shows
Fresher — unlike all others I have seen.

The "beings of the mind," though "not of
     clay" —
   "Essentially immortal,"[1] and "a joy
   Forever"[2] — even these may pall and cloy,
For all that poets gloriously say.

[1] "The beings of the mind are not of clay : Essentially immortal," etc. — Byron.
[2] "A thing of beauty is a joy forever." — Keats.

Yea, and thy own charms, Nature, when por-
    trayed
  By hand of man, become the spoil of time.
  The seasons mar, not change them : in sublime
Repose they reign — but evermore to fade.

Whence comes, then, thy perennial youth re-
    newed ?
  Thy freshness, as of everlasting morn ?
  God's breath is on thee.   Of it thou wast born,
And with its fragrance is thy life bedewed.

Nor can I need aught sterner than thy face
  To wean me from the things that pass away.
  Not by autumnal lesson of decay,
Or vernal hymn of renovating grace ;

But by this fragrance of the Infinite :
  For here my soul catches her native air ;
  And tastes the ever fresh, the ever fair,
That wait her in the Gardens of Delight.

CHOICE IN NO CHOICE

I KNOW not which to love the more:
  The morning with its liquid light;
Or evening with its tender lore
  Of silver lake and purple height.

To morn I say, " The fairer thou:
  For when thy beauties melt away,
'Tis but to breathe on heart and brow
  The gladness of the perfect day."

And o'er the water falls a hue
  That feasts, but cannot sate, the eye.
'Twould seem our Lady's mantle threw
  Its glory from an upper sky.

But when has glared the torrid noon,
  And afternoon is gasping low,
The sunset brings a sweeter boon
  Than ever graced the Orient's glow.

And I : " As old wine unto new,
  Art thou to morn, belovèd eve!
And what if dies thy every hue
  In blankest night ? We may not grieve.

" Thy fading lulls us as we dote.
   Nor always blank the genial night:
For when the moon is well afloat,
   Thou mellowest into amber light."

Is each, then, fairer in its turn?
   'Tis hence the music.   Not for me
To wish a dayless morn, or yearn
   For nightless eve — if these could be.

But give me both — the new, the old:
   And let my spirit sip the wine
From silver now, and now from gold:
   'Tis wine alike — alike divine.

SUGGESTED BY A CASCADE

I

NOT idly could I watch this torrent fall
   Hour after hour: not vainly day by day
   Visit the spot to meditate and pray.
The charm that holds me in its giant thrall
Has too much of the Infinite to pall.
   For tho', like time, the waters pass away,
   They fling a freshness, a baptismal spray,

Which breathes of the Eternal Fount of all.
And so, my God, does Thy revealèd Word
   In living dogma, or on sacred page —
Flow to us ever new; tho' read and heard
   Immutably the same from age to age.
   And thither Nature sends us to assuage
The higher longings by her voices stirred.

II

Those voices, like the one I listen here —
   Tho' blending evermore, as tone with tone —
   Are each a perfect music : each, alone,
A faultless melody even to the ear;
But to the heart a mystery as dear
   As the unutter'd meanings of its own.
   And other sweet monotonies, unknown
To all but Catholic hearts, sound year by year,
And day by day, yet weary not.   The song
   Of Holy Church, her Mass, her Vespers, flow,
Like this clear stream, unchangingly along;
   Nor newer seem'd a thousand years ago.
   Then where the proof great Nature's self can
      show,
Of source Divine, more exquisitely strong ?

LAKE GEORGE, 1875.

AN EARNEST

THE world is ever to the child
    The same as when on me it smiled
And thrill'd a bosom undefiled:

Its freshness evermore renewed
With sunny morn, and flowers bedewed,
And light-wing'd joys to be pursued.

Then Spring was all, and darling May;
And thro' the Summer's sweet delay
The Golden Age regained its sway:

While Autumn came with thankless pace,
And yielded with a sullen grace
To Winter's hard, relentless face.

A change: and these had welcome grown,
As friends of calmer, deeper tone,
Whose thoughts anticipate our own:

While those mov'd dreamlike in the vast,
With vanish'd hopes too bright to last
And memories of a purer past.

I said : " When I have done with earth,
Will that first joy seem nothing worth,
Or know a second, larger, birth ? "

I ween the answer tarried long :
But when it came 'twas clear and strong,
Tho' softer than a linnet's song :

The voice of Faith, forbidding doubt ;
The voice of Nature round about ;
The voice of God — within, without.

" Your conscious heart has told you sooth,
That you regain'd, in gaining Truth,
A freshness better than of youth.

" What need you, then, of hint or view,
More than this foretaste of the dew
That falls where God ' makes all things new ' ? "

ST. HERMENEGILD

A Passion Flower of Spain

INTRODUCTION

WHILE a guest of the Lazarist Fathers in Santiago, Chile, in the year 1888, I found in their library a Spanish work very like our Butler's " Lives of the Saints." Having for years entertained the idea suggested by the venerable friend to whose memory I inscribe the realization, I took notes from the book just mentioned regarding this martyr of old Spain. These notes, together with St. Gregory's short story given in the Roman Breviary, appeared sufficient data for a narrative poem. Accordingly, I planned one of about half the length of my present attempt; but one which would have been, as I afterwards discovered, considerably at variance with historic fact.

It was not until a year ago last January that I found time to do much at my poem: and when I was nearing the end of it, it occurred to me that I had better consult the Bollandists

— their ponderous tomes being at hand (in this our Pittsburgh monastery). To my surprise, I found that the time which elapsed between Leovigild's declaration of war and the martyrdom of St. Hermenegild was six years instead of three; that while some authors made it three, they were inaccurate, the date of Easter at the time of the martyrdom settling the year beyond dispute. Consequently, I had to change my plan and divide the story into two parts. But I found no leisure for finishing the poem until the present year.

I have, of course, used the license accorded to poets and romancers, but within, as I think, very reasonable bounds. The incident of my hero sending wife and child to Africa I took from the Spanish " Lives " aforesaid.

With regard to the name of my Saint, I keep the form of it which is undoubtedly the Gothic original. It is not so musical, perhaps, as " Ermengild," or even " Hermigild,"—modern forms I have seen; but I believe in using the name found in the Roman Martyrology. The *g*, let me remark, is hard. The name of my heroine is given as " Ingun*dis* " by the Bollandists, but as "Ingun*da*" by the Spanish historian : and since "Gosvind*a*" is the only form of the other lady's name in either work, I conclude that Gothic names of women admitted of the Latin termination.

St. Paul's Monastery,
Pittsburgh, Pa., March, 1896.

ST. HERMENEGILD

PART I

I

L EOVIGILD, the Arian king of Spain,
    Had warr'd upon the Roman faith, and
    driven
Its Greek adherents off the settled coasts.
Then, planning boldly, in his pride of heart,
To make the crown hereditary and keep
Succession with his line, he raised his sons,
Hermenegild and Reccared, to share
Barbaric splendors of the Visigoth sway :
Bestowing Andalusia's rich domain
On Prince Hermenegild — first-born, best lov'd;
To Reccared the realm of Arragon
Assigning, with the provinces that lay
'Twixt Ebro and the Pyrenean wall.

Of Catholic mother came the princes twain :
And sore, I ween, had Theodosia griev'd
To see them rear'd in heresy. For well
She lov'd her faith. But, blent with mother's
    tears,

The mother's prayers went upward day and
    night;
Returning in a dew of grace that fed
The seed she had planted in each childhood's
    breast, —
A Catholic love and reverence for the names
Of Jesus and of Mary.   Thus she lived,
Sowing in tears to one day reap in joy.
Whereof was earnest sent her at her death,
What time her brother Leander came himself—
A saintly prelate he of Christ's one flock —
Ay, came himself to robe her soul for flight,
Leovigild conniving.   "Fear thou not,
My sister," quoth the saint.   "Thy task is
    o'er.
Like Magdalen, what thou couldest thou hast
    done.
The day thy summons found me, while I stood
Holding aloft the consecrated Host
With wonted thought of thee, I heard a voice
Within me; and, in vision of the mind,
Beheld two champions chosen to restore
The true faith's glory to our Spain, and one
To reign upon her altars for all time.
Thy sons, my sister.   Thou, like Monica,

Hast brought them forth a second time — to
    God."
And so this "valiant woman" died in peace.

But soon Leovigild, with tearless eyes,
Look'd round for other consort, and espoused
Gosvinda, widow of Athanagild,
And sharer in his own perverted creed.
Then, bent to find Hermenegild a bride,
Obtained Ingunda's hand — a princess famed
No less for virtue than for beauty : ay,
And richer far with faith's high dower than
    aught
Of gold or gems could make her.
                        Daughter she
To Sigisbert the Frank and Brunechild,
Child of Gosvinda; for whose sake, in sooth,
Leovigild had made reluctant choice.
"I know her," urged the vixen. "She is soft
As wax to skilful hands. Leave all to me.
A year in this our palace, at the most,
And, trust me, thou wilt see her change for truth
Her Roman superstition, like a dress."
And so they met — the bridegroom and the
    bride —

One April day.   And straightway, all his heart
Went out to her, and all her heart to him.

II

A moon past sweetly o'er the bridal pair
Within the imperial city, where the flock
Of Peter, thronging their one suffer'd church,
Had hail'd the prince's nuptials as a pledge
Of coming freedom : so assured were they,
Knowing his kindly nature, he would prove
Their advocate, and stay his father's hand.

Meanwhile Hermenegild, from day to day
Increased in love and reverence for a spouse
So pure, so gentle; and Ingunda prayed
That God's dear grace might lead him to the
        light —
The choicest blessing she could ask for one
So worthy perfect trust.   But not for long
This happy season.   Ere the second moon
Had left the crescent, pale Gosvinda's hate,
Till now dissembled well, made clouds, and
        threw
A shadow over peace.
                              Leovigild,

On whom his daughter's loveliness had wrought
A softening spell, but frown'd, and coldly said:
" Tush! Let her pray. What harm such
    women's prayers?
Hermenegild holds truly that, to ween
Our Roman subjects from seditious thought,
'Tis wiser to be mild and merciful."
" Ay!" cried Gosvinda, " and when comes the
    babe?
Nor one alone, be sure. Such women bear
As well as pray." Quoth he: " The babe is
    ours.
'Twill be but Theodosia once again.
She bore me sons, and could not choose but
    yield
Her offspring to the holy Arian cause.
But whence art *thou* so zealous for the cause,
With thy two daughters wed to Catholic kings?"

So, flushing shame, and swallowing the hot word,
Gosvinda turn'd in bitter scorn, and vow'd
Swift conquest of Ingunda. Whom she plied
With hints of royal displeasure; then with
    threats
Of exile from the husband of her love.

At these Ingunda smiled : such trust had she
Her mate would follow wheresoe'er she went,
Ev'n should he lose a kingdom for her sake.
And once she spoke of refuge and defence —
Her father Sigisbert, the Catholic king :
Whereat Gosvinda, letting loose the fiend
Within her, fell upon the sweet young wife,
And dragg'd her by the hair, and beat her sore.

Now, twice and thrice, the meek Ingunda took
This outrage as a welcome drop of gall
From out her Saviour's chalice, and besought
The Virgin-Mother for her tender aid
In strength of silence.   But it timely chanced
That Prince Hermenegild, with soon return
Gosvinda guess'd not, suddenly came where
          lay,
Torn, bleeding, and in swoon of seeming death,
His heart's belovèd.
                    " Ha! some woman's work
Is here ! " quoth he.   And when the sum-
          mon'd maids
Had help'd revive their mistress, and he said
" Go, tell the Queen that I would speak with
          her,"

And drew for answer " The Queen keeps her
    room
Till evening "— straightway the divining thought
Flash'd into knowledge. Then, dismiss'd the
    maids,
With solemn charge of secrecy, he knelt
Beside his bride's recumbent form, and kiss'd
Her face and hands, and sooth'd her tenderly.

" My dearest, with thy perfect love and trust
(Which well I know), how couldst thou hide a
    wrong
Not born, I ween, to-day, nor yesterday ?
For twice and thrice have I observ'd a pain
In the blue eyes, and round the timid mouth ;
Yet thou didst meet my question with a smile
That made me think thy meditation ran
On that new image of the Crucified
I hear of — yonder, in the church. But now
The cause is clear. Without one word of thine,
I know the wretch, whate'er her motive be —
Fanatic zeal, or jealous spite, or both —
Has dared to lay her sacrilegious hands
On my Ingunda. And I blame myself
For not withdrawing sooner. We will go

To where my princedom's capital awaits
The presence of its ruler. Fear thou naught.
'Twill take but little to persuade the King."

But she made answer: " Husband of my heart,
My prayer is granted. Now thou knowest all.
But breathe not, I beseech thee, to the King
Gosvinda's conduct. For right sure am I
He dreams not of it. He has ever shown
A father's kindness tow'rd me, for thy sake.
Nor bear Gosvinda malice. We should pray
For those that wrong us. Calmly let us go."
Then, with her true arms twined about his neck:
" O my belovèd, 'twill be sweet indeed
To reign with thee in Hispalis ! The Queen
Talk'd exile at me — banishment from thee.
I smil'd, supremely happy in the thought
That thou wouldst surely fly to me afar,
If forfeiting a kingdom. Such my trust."
And he — could only seal it with his lips.

III

" Calm as thy stream, O Bœtis, flows my life:
But ah, how soon thy waters reach the sea —
There to be lost in evermore unrest ! . . .

The sea — what means this strange presentiment
That yet 'twill roll between my love and
    me ? . . .
Begone, sad thought !   For all is gladness now.
The bishop has at last return'd — at last
(Again forgive, Lord, my impatient heart):
And I have seen him, told him all.   My Prince
Has promised to receive him graciously ;
Nor only as his mother's brother, him
Who stood beside her death-bed, bringer of
    peace ;
But also as a lover of the poor,
And one of whom the very Arians here
Report but kindly.   Ere to-morrow's noon
They meet."
        'Twas thus Ingunda voiced her thought
In Hispalis, one August afternoon ;
Reposing in a favorite arbor, where
The terraced garden look'd upon the river :
And saw the morrow prove a golden day —
A day long pray'd for, but of larger fruit
Than brightest hope had ripen'd while she pray'd.

They met — Leander, prelate, saint, and sage,
And he, the chivalrous Prince : but not to hold

The talk of polish'd insincerity.
First greetings done, the Prince, revering more
The uncle who had cheer'd his mother's death
Than aught of churchly dignity, avow'd
His ever-mindful gratitude, and past
To speak of other merits in his guest —
As watchful pastor, father of the poor.
Whereat Leander courage took to plead
For royal protection in his flock's behalf:
Nor merely gain'd a promise, easily given
And easily broken, or a smooth reply
Which meant as little as it cost: but while
The young man gaz'd upon the old man's face,
He saw a peace there he had ne'er beheld
With priest or prelate of his sect — a light
That blent morn's hope with evening's perfect
        rest —
And felt a ray let in upon his soul.
Then, putting off the prince, drew near, and
        said,
With look and pose of reverent earnestness:
" Father — so let me call thee — since thy
        coming,
I know not why, but I have seem'd as one
Born in a palace underground, and kept

From any light but garish lamps, and taught
That all without was dimmer light, or dark :
To whom steals down a messenger of good,
Bringing the truth and breathing round a sense
Of light and fragrance from the genial day."

"The day indeed, my son.   Now, God be
    praised ! "
The saint made answer — ere his heart well'd up,
Choking his utterance.   Then Hermenegild
Knelt suddenly before him, caught his hand
And kiss'd it.   But Leander, blessing him,
Said quickly : " Rise, my son.   Not now, not
    here.
Come to me where in secret I may guide
Thy soul, and feed it with the truth it craves.
'Tis prudence bids me caution.   I forebode
Naught to myself, but much, my Prince, to thee.
No shame in prudence.   Maybe, thou hast
    heard
How Nicodemus came to Christ by night :
And did the Master chide him for his fear ? "

So came by stealth Hermenegild, to learn
From Him whom favor'd Nicodemus heard.

For, hearing now Leander, he heard Christ;
And, hearing Christ, the Father, who had sent,
His Co-Eternal, Consubstantial Word
To dwell made flesh among us, and to teach
With human lips the Truth which giveth life.
And sweetly flow'd this life into his soul,
As eagerly listen'd the delighted Prince
To that most restful mystery of faith,
One God in Persons Three — all God in each —
Indissoluble Oneness.   Now was clear,
What oft before had teas'd him as he thought,
How God could dwell alone eternally,
A boundless happiness within Himself,
And need no creature's love.   No creature, then,
His Son, the Christ; but very God of God
Begotten : nor He through whom the Mother-
    Maid
Conceiv'd : but She true Spouse, true Mother,
    of God.

IV

" Incomparable fact, that God is man !
The great Creator His own creature's Son !
Omnipotence a babe !   What, after this,
Is hard to faith ?   What left for wonderment ?"

So mus'd Hermenegild, baptized, and seal'd
The self-same hour with the confirming Chrism;
And waiting for the morrow, to be fed
With that Divine Food which is Christ Himself.

To whom Leander, full of thankful love:
" Yes, one thing still is left for wonderment :
The Passion.   Not so much that God should die,
Once born a mortal : but that He should drink
The very wine of pain; should yield His flesh
To mangling scourge, His head to thorny crown;
Be jeer'd at for a knave ; mock'd for a fool;
Struck face and mouth, and spurn'd, and spit
    upon ;
Take sentence to a slave's, a felon's, death;
Carry shame's cross in company with thieves;
And die as one accursèd ! . . .   Is not this
Surpassing wonderful ? "

               "Yet," quoth the Prince,
Royal-hearted, " could the King of kings do
    less,
In stooping to a Passion for our sakes,
Than go the possible farthest ?   Wring from
    pain
And shame and insult the last bitter drop,

Then drain and suck the cup, and cry 'I thirst!'
Unsated?   This, to me, seems worthiest God.

" And what can *we*, in turn, do less than ask
To suffer for *His* sake?   I envy those —
Thy brethren, and now mine in common faith —
Who have felt my blinded father's heavy arm:
Tho' mine shall be the task to stem his wrath
And turn it — Ay, I envy them; and most,
Whom death has crown'd with victory.   And
        if I " —

" Prince," said Leander quickly, " well I know
Thy thought.   And 'tis, in sooth, a noble greed
That covets martyrdom.   But thine, my son,
Another charity for Christ; nor less
Of cost, — but more — in patient fortitude.
Bethink thyself — thus early raised to share
Imperial power, and timely led to truth —
A chosen instrument in mercy's hand
To work a people's rescue.   And for this
Is needed more than hero's courage, more
Than statesman's prudence.   Thou must seek
        to gain

Thy royal sire, with all thy kith and kin,
By argument of pure and gentle life,
Waiting God's hidden moments : even as she
Whom *His* grace gave thee, rather than the
      King's,
Hath now her waiting's joyous recompense.
How much thou owest to her faithful prayers!
One day shall others owe as much to thine."

With this he blest the kneeling Prince, and
      went :
But with a haste unwonted, and a brow
Which ill conceal'd the trouble deep within.

" It must be so ! " he murmur'd when alone.
" My heart foreboded truly.   I have striven
To keep his thoughts — in this, perchance, to
      blame —
Away from that extreme of sacrifice
Whither they tend by what I now perceive
An impulse all divine.   I would not prove
Another Caiphas ; yet come the words
Of that arch-schemer aptly to my lips —
' 'Tis well that one man for the nation die.'

Let God fulfil His purpose.   Mine the part
Of prayer and preparation : yea, and more
For my weak self, methinks, than ev'n for him,
My neophyte.   For if I may but share
The palm with him, how undeserv'd a joy ! "

V

But tranquilly as yet Hermenegild
Enjoy'd his new-found faith: the while his
    spouse
Look'd onward to an anxious hour, and pray'd
That the young soul within her might arrive
The gate of birth, which only leads to death,
And, safely passing, reach that other birth
Which is the gate of life.
                Nor vainly pray'd
Ingunda, till her husband knew the joy
Of holding to his heart a son and heir.
Ah, innocent babe — and can it be that thou,
Dear pledge of benediction, sent to crown
Thy parents' love, wilt bring them cruel woe?
Little, I trow, the mother dreamt of grief —
Too rapt in bliss that only mothers know.

But soon Hermenegild betray'd his thought
By silent mood and look of stern resolve:
Resolve heroically strengthen'd, when
Leander, summon'd to the palace, gave
Counsel as stern, tho' calm withal and sweet.

" God save thee!   Loud the acclamations ring,
From town and hamlet, that 'a prince is born —
An heir to the new throne of Hispalis!'
All thought of creed forgotten for the nonce:
Yet not with priest and prelate of the sect.
Their Arian malice, ever on the watch,
Erects its venomous head, and waits to strike.

" Thou sayest 'Let it strike!   The time has
      come
For open avowal.   It were base to hide
The full truth longer.'   Even so, my son.
Thy true heart *here* no counsel needs of mine.
Thy subjects all shall see their sovereign's heir
Baptized right solemnly in the Catholic faith.
But mark me: one of two things follow — flight
Or war.   For swiftly will the message go
To rouse Leovigild — incredulous yet,
But warn'd, and smarting from Gosvinda's taunts.
And here thy heart *doth* counsel need of mine.

A sudden journey, such as Joseph took
To Egypt, with the Virgin and her Child,
Is not, alas! for thee.   But thou canst send,
With ample guard, the Princess and the babe
On visit to her father Sigisbert:
Thyself awaiting letters from the King,
And pleading with him as a son should plead;
Meanwhile, if this be fruitless, gaining time
To countervail his measures."
                                    Bow'd the Prince
In loving reverence; and simply said:
" Enough, my father.   Be thy counsel taken.
'Tis God who guideth thee."
                                    And bright the morn
Which saw the royal babe new-born to life
Eternal, with the name Theodoric.
Great was the feasting: deep the joy of all
Within the Fold; while few of those without
But shared the dance, the viands, and the wine,
With equal zest; indifferent to the loss,
Which some resented, to the Arian cause.

VI

But now the reptile head, in act to strike,
No longer paused.   If swiftly to the King

Ran couriers from his son, a greeting fair
Of filial love and pride paternal bearing,
As swiftly sped the messengers of hate.
And soon came back a letter to the Prince,
Of most undoubtful meaning.

      "Son," it said, —
" My first-born, pride and hope of many years —
Thy timely message, that is born to thee
A son and heir, fell coldly on my heart,
By reason of another word, that kept
Swift pace with thine : yet so incredible,
That I withhold belief till thou thyself
Confirm it. Hast thou weakly yielded, son,
To thy young wife's persuasion, and allow'd
A Roman prelate to baptize thy child ?
If so, what wonder that our Arian priests
Declare thyself perverted from the faith ?
Now, write me, speedily, the very truth :
That I may *know*, and knowing act."

        The Prince
Made answer thus : " My King, my father, know
The very truth. God's mercy, undeserv'd,
Has call'd me out of darkness into light.
My sweet young wife has no persuasion used,

Nor other influence than her constant prayer
To Heaven.   Blame not her, nor yet my lord
Leander, my dead mother's brother.   Chide
Myself alone, if chide thou must.   But know
That I am still thy loyal subject, still
Thy loving son, who only asks to keep
His new-found faith in peace.   Let truth be free,
Since truth alone can make her bondsmen free.
And if thou doubt my hold upon the truth,
As now I know it, see what I have risk'd
For its dear sake : and trust me, when I say
That I am ready to lose throne and crown,
And wife and child, — yea, life itself — for Him
Whom now I worship as my Lord and God,
Second in Consubstantial Trinity."

Now, in his secret heart, Leovigild
Was mov'd by this high courage of his son
To admiration and a pact of peace.
But pale Gosvinda, plying him with threats
Of ripe rebellion she herself had plann'd —
Feigning it learnt from confidence betray'd
By over-trusted women of her suite —
So wrought upon him that he suddenly sent
This stern rejoinder :

"If, in thirty days,
Our son and subject, Prince Hermenegild,
Have not abjured the creed of Rome, and sworn
To live himself, and rear his infant heir,
True to his country's faith : then, let him know
We judge him traitor, and will visit him —
An army at our back.   Thus saith the King."

VII

" He gives me thirty days. 'Tis well.   But thou
Must fly, my darling, with our little one !
And I have plann'd the whither ; but must seek
Leander first, and get his benison,
Before I break the doleful news to thee."
Thus to himself Hermenegild.   And when
Leander, radiant with a prayer-caught light,
Had read the sullen mandate of the King,
And heard the young man's scheme, he gave at
    once
His sanction and his blessing, with a word
Prophetic.   " Be it so, belovèd son.
Ingunda and the child will safely reach
That shore, and yet another, where thyself
Shalt give them Easter joy."   Whereat the
    Prince,

Forbearing further question, craved the boon
Of his good uncle's presence and support,
The better to prepare his tender wife
For swift and cruel parting.

      Her they found
Watching the cradled slumbers of her boy,
And musing on that Queen of womanhood,
The Virgin-Mother with her Babe Divine.

" My daughter," said Leander, " thou hast heard
Of Herod's rage, and Joseph's sudden flight,
With Mary and her Child, to heathen land.
In God's mysterious counsel, a decree
Of exile — 'twill be brief — must now go forth,
Bidding *thee* fly from heresy's mad rage,
And take thy infant to a friendly shore.
Alas, without thy Joseph !   But not long
Wilt have to bear this parting, as I trust.
I see an Easter morning — when the Prince
Shall glad thine eyes, crown'd victor from the
  fight."

No scream : no swoon. But, falling on her knees
Beside her babe, she bent her comely head,
And murmur'd : " Fiat, O my Father, fiat !

Fiat voluntas tua, O my God!"
Then silent wept. Whereat Hermenegild
Knelt too, to soothe her. And Leander blest
The stricken pair, and offer'd them to Him
Who, in His wondrous love, for them Himself
Had offer'd — in the crib, and on the Cross.
The bishop blest them for a moment; then
Slipt softly from the room, and left them there
Unconscious he had gone.
                                    But soon the Prince,
Arising from his knees, all gently raised
His drooping bride, and held her to his heart.
" My own sweet love, so nobly brave thou art,
I need not hesitate to tell thee all.
Come, sit beside me on this couch the while,
And lean thy head upon a faithful breast.

" The King has granted me but thirty days
To yield submissively myself and heir
To live for what he calls our country's faith,
Abjuring that of Rome. To plead were vain.
I know his spirit. Rather would he brook
Defiance than a craven suit for pity.
I wis, he fears rebellion, and the loss
Of kingdom : thinking that the Arian Church

Has power to overthrow him. I will prove
That here his quiet has been play'd upon.

" Then why must thou, belovèd, flee his wrath —
Thou and our infant son ? Because he comes
(So reads the message) after thirty days,
An army at his back. Nay, tremble not,
My darling." " 'Tis for thee." " Nor yet for
    me.
I too can raise an army : and our cause
Is just — the cause of Truth — the cause of
    Christ.
My people love me : and the King will find
My Arians choose between us in a way
He little dreams of.
              But the plan of flight.
Whither shalt go ? Where hide our little one ?
Leander spoke before of Sigisbert,
Thy father; who could shield thee well. But
    now
Thou couldst not thither hie and shun pursuit,
I fear me. So another plan is mine.
Among our subjects here in Hispalis,
A stalwart son of Holy Church, and one
Whom God has prosper'd in extensive trade,

Has frequent traffic with the Roman towns
On Afric's coast.   In one a mansion owns;
Residing now on this shore, now on that.
He, having friends at court, and learning thence
Gosvinda's triumph in the threat of war,
Came privily, ere closed the second day
That follow'd the despatch, and nobly made
An offer of his house beyond the sea!
His wife and three young daughters winter there;
And wait to show thee loyal welcome, love,
While guarding well the secret of thy rank.
Their servants will be thine: thou needest take
But one handmaiden and Theodoric's nurse.
Our holy Church is there, too; and thy soul
Will find religion's comfort, even as here.

" Wilt go, then, dearest ?   For a goodly ship
Lies in the river, ready to convey
Thyself and babe to safety and to rest.
You go aboard by night, and sail at dawn:
Thus baffling prowlers, maybe, on the watch
To seize our child — anticipating flight
Tow'rd Sigisbert's dominions.   Wilt thou go?"
" Yea, husband of my heart: thy will is mine;
For surely it is God's.   To-morrow night?"

"Amen.   And keep Leander's cheering words
Fresh in thy memory.   Whether few the weeks,
Or many, till the promised Easter morn,
That man of God had caught a light in prayer.
But if this coming Easter pass us by
Still parted, then shall Heaven's kind breezes waft
My darling to her native shore: and there
Her childhood's home will guard her till we
      meet."

END OF PART I

ST. HERMENEGILD

PART II

THE thirty days pass'd quickly. But the
Prince
Had visited the Roman camp, and gain'd
A promise of support — too lightly given,
Had he but noted. Then to all his towns
Had gone himself, or trusty spokesmen sent,
To state his cause and prove it one of peace —
Religious peace, and conscience' sacred rights:
To all proclaiming fullest liberty
To hold and worship as it seem'd them good.
" His sire, Leovigild, in evil hour,
Had listen'd to a voice that counsell'd hate.
Religion should be love. And if the King,
Hardening his heart, as Pharao did of yore,
Should bring the curse of war on loyal son
And faithful subjects, then with *him* must rest
The guilt; with him the dread account; and fall
On him the sentence of the Sovran Judge."

So now he sent his answer to the King:
Nor wasting love, nor showing sign of fear.

" His subjects all were with him, quite content
Beneath his rule's light yoke.   Leovigild
Might   come   himself   and   question   thro'   the
      land.
The Roman captains had approv'd his course,
Unsheathing   friendly   swords.   His   wife   and
      child
Were far from danger's reach.
                              While hoping still
That wiser counsels might avail to change
The King's intent, yet firmer his resolve
And firmer grew, to battle for God's truth,
If need should be — ay, even unto death.

" But thou, my Sire, canst thou, in turn, speak
      thus —
Tho' well persuaded thine a righteous cause ?
Art waging war on thine own flesh and blood
From greater dearness of eternal truth ?
Nor, rather, from a most unworthy fear
Of swift dethronement by a pamper'd Church —
Thy Church, not mine ?
                              Enough, I leave thee now,
With   steadfast   prayer,   to   conscience   and   to
      God."

But came no further message from the King;
Nor any sound of arms.   Hermenegild
Hoped greatly for a space; yet, undeceiv'd,
Went on preparing for long siege of war,
Knowing his father's suddenness of mood.
But little guess'd the generous-hearted Prince —
Of whom, in sooth (most happily for him),
The mother's nature had the larger share —
That proud Leovigild would stoop to craft,
Or deign the basest of all weapons use,
The potency of faith-corrupting gold.

II

Bright Easter, gladdest feast of all the year,
Some earnest brought of triumph and of rest
To our young hero: but Leander's word,
'Twas plain, yet lack'd fulfilment many a moon.
So, first, to Sigisbert, the Frankish king,
By trusty couriers from the Roman camp,
The Prince sent word: detailing clear and full
The persecution and Ingunda's flight.
He ask'd not help — save only that of prayer;
But to the father of his well-belov'd
Confided tenderly herself and child,
For safest keeping till the war should end.

Then, for his bride the same good ship dispatch'd
Had borne her faithfully to Afric's shore.
And thus he wrote:
                    "One Easter morn has past;
And much I fear another, and another,
Will see us parted still.   But thou, belov'd,
My dearer life, shalt now abide once more
Safe in thy childhood's home which thou didst
        leave
For me.
                    Leovigild has made no sign
Of onset; but his sullen silence tells
How little he had reckon'd on a front
Defiant, such as we have dared to show.
Leander warns me that the King will try
Vexatious tarrying, and will use beside
Dishonorable means, which I refuse
To credit him withal.   But we, the while,
Avail ourselves of time."
                    Leander spoke
Too truly.   For a dozen months roll'd by,
And no invasion of the Prince's realm;
Save that of spies and secret agents, sent
To sow false fears, to wheedle, and to bribe.
And saw the sequent year a bolder move,

But deftly hidden from our hero's eyes.
The Roman captains privately receiv'd
A courteous invitation from the King
To spend a week within Tolétum's walls:
Departing thence the richer by a sum
Of yellow gold, with guaranty of more.
Small reck to them, I ween, that they had sold
Honor and plighted faith. The King but
    ask'd
Neutrality: and what had they to do
With family broils and petty jars of creed?

But kept for the third year his master-stroke
This Visigoth king. Magnificently royal
The edict summoning to his capital
The Arian prelates of all Spain.
                        Convened,
The council sat in state, encompass'd round
With awe-compelling pomp and pageantry,
His Majesty presiding. Ay, and long
Had been the disputation, long and fierce,
But for the gold that won astuter minds
To sanction novel measures of the King's.
And first, 'twas carried that the Arian Church
Should own Rome's baptism a valid act,

Nor re-baptize the converts from her fold.[1]
And next, that she admitted and believ'd
Equality 'twixt the Father and the Son —
Left ample room for sense heretical.[2]
Thus artfully contrived Leovigild
What rightly he had guess'd would undermine
The seeming strong position of his son.
A hope, by Heaven's high permit, realized.

III

For now began the onset.   Came the King,
A well-appointed army at his back,
To pay his promised visit.   Marching straight
On Hispalis, he drew the lines of siege;
While up the Bœtis sail'd a stately fleet,
To cut off access from the sea and cause
A gradual famine in the leaguer'd town.
The Prince's ships were taken all, or sunk —
Outnumber'd, overpower'd.   But Hispalis
Smiled bravely on the foe a round of months;

---

[1] *Vide* Bollandists.   In his "Essay on Development," Cardinal Newman tells us that the Arian Visigoths had an invalid form of baptism themselves, but re-baptized by force all the Catholics they could get hold of.

[2] "Equality" not necessarily including co-eternity and consubstantiality.

For strong her walls : and, strangely, not a feint
Of storm was made.   Yet, secretly, within,
Work'd treachery — unscented by the Prince,
And all too late detected by his friends.
He had not seconded Leander's wish
To stay with the besieged ; and sadly missed
The holy bishop's prudence.

                      Easter dawn'd
Again : the fourth since sweet Ingunda's flight.
Alas, 'twas silence now between those hearts !
No word might come or go.   But many words
Had framed an answering letter prompt and true
To one had reach'd the Princess at her home.
And this Hermenegild read o'er and o'er.

" I live in hope," she said, " unshaken hope ;
And know that peace which is the gift of God
To those who love Him, and, to prove their love,
Are well content to suffer for His sake.
Three years of parted life have only knit
Our mutual souls more tenderly and more.
And if another three be God's dear will,
We shall but gain in merit and in love.
Nor are we parted save to outer sense :
For since in God ' we live and move and be,'

In Him I have thee with me at all hours.
And when, at Holy Mass, our Lord and King
Comes to His altar, *thou* art nearer then;
For in His Heart He keeps thee, well I know:
And nearest when that Heart is one with mine
In blest Communion. . . .

       I have taught our child
To lisp thy name, belov'd, and softly pray
At morn, at eve, thy safety, thy return.
And he, betimes, will ask for thee, and pause
As tho' he heard an angel answer him!" . . .

Pored fondly on these sentences, and oft,
The tender husband: but on those which urged
That he should take, if worsted in the war,
Safe refuge with her father, look'd but once.
So, when his captains brought him sudden news
Of widespread disaffection ev'n among
The Catholic soldiers — weary of his cause,
And bought with golden promises convey'd
By sham deserters from the enemy's lines —
He cast Ingunda's letter to the flames;
And straightway steel'd his heart for doom and
   death,
Rather than base alternative of flight.

Then, counsel taken with his faithful chiefs,
Made noiseless exit under cover of night,
And reached the Roman camp. His thought to
    claim
The pledg'd support, and place at its command
Two hosts which lay inactive, north and south,
Protecting towns and hamlets unassail'd.
This junction formed, the siege were quickly
    raised ;
Th' invader forced back to his own domain.

Brave, noble heart, and true God-fearing soul,
How keen thine anguish now ! How bitter the cup
Press'd to thy lips !   And thou must drink it
    down —
Ay, drain the very dregs !
                    The lust of gold
Had play'd i' the game, and won.   With cold
    salute,
The Romans talk'd of sworn neutrality.
But this they offer'd still : asylum sure,
Or armèd escort to the bounds of Gaul.
He turn'd, indignant, to retrace his steps ;
And tidings met that Hispalis had fallen —
Her gates flung open by the glad besieged !

IV

The Prince had still two armies in the field;
And cities twain, strong, Catholic, and loyal,
Could long resistance make. So thus he plann'd.
The King should think him fled to Corduba;
Pursue, and find his late-exultant host
Between two armies caught. Himself, the
    while,
First choosing out three hundred valiant men,
Would hold Ossétum.
              But Leovigild —
At all times wary, never more than now —
By spies in part, in part by traitors' aid,
Saw thro' his son's manœuvre, and abode
In Andalusia's capital, unbeguiled.
Then weeks and months of dallying, dextrous
    feints,
And moves strategic; till he drew apart
Each rebel corps; and, summoning their chiefs
To parley, urged, 'gainst useless waste of blood,
His generous intent toward every man
Should lay down arms and heed his gracious
    will.
" For well he knew that motives high and pure

Had bade them follow his misguided son.
He blamed not *them*.   In proof whereof, to each
Would royal largess give of double pay
For unrequited service to the Prince."
Thus either host disbanded and dispersed
Like phantom armies seen in summer clouds.

Now, vulture-like, he swoopt upon the walls
Of doom'd Ossétum.   Sending to inform
The obdurate Prince of his deserted cause,
He offer'd clemency and all the grace
A father's heart could give.   But who shall blame
Our hero, if distrustfully he heard,
And answer'd from amid his Spartan few,
That, sooner than abandon faith and God,
'Twere better to die fighting in the breach
And fall a martyr?
                    The three hundred made
Round their Leonidas a glorious stand,
When fell the batter'd gates.   Ay, then was seen
" A new Thermopylæ." [1]   Again, again,

---

[1] " Earth, render back from out thy breast
     A remnant of our Spartan dead !
     Of the Three Hundred grant but three,
     To make a new Thermopylæ ! "
                    — Byron's " Isles of Greece."

Bristled with spear and javelin surge on surge,
Recoiling baffled, broken. Till, at last,
A shower of arrows from the mounted wall
Laid low the brave defenders — all but ten.

The wounded Prince beheld a flood of light,
And angels bringing for each fallen head
A martyr's crown. But ah, not yet for him!
He heard a voice: " Prince, hie thee to the
      church!
'Tis not the will of Heaven thou finish here
Thy combat. Waits a brighter crown for thee."
That light the while seem'd darkness to the foe,
And gave the little band secure retreat.

V

Now, when Leovigild had full report
Of his son's valor 'mid the hero throng
Who fought and fell around him, he was thrill'd
With pride paternal; and at once enjoin'd
Respect for the asylum's sacred walls.
And that mysterious darkness aw'd his soul.
Then, sending flag of truce at eventide,
With food and drink, and bandages for wounds,
He queried was the Prince's hurt severe?

And would he on the morrow deign receive
His brother Reccared ?
                    The Prince was touch'd
By this strange show of kindliness, and made
A like response.   Not grave his wound, nor
      those
Of his nine comrades.   Gratefully they took
The timely alms.   Ay, let his brother come.
" I have not seen him since the blessèd day
I wed Ingunda," mused Hermenegild.
" So *he* is in the field against me !   *He*
Takes sides with Arian hate!   But nay.   I ween
The King has brought him but to plead with me.
Ay, let him come.   We will embrace and speak
Of our lost mother and her precious faith."
Thus ran, 'twixt intervals of feverish sleep,
His thoughts.   And much he pray'd the coming
      day
Might see him win his brother to the truth.

A happy meeting.   If the younger Prince,
Invested with the pomp of embassy,
Forbore to rush into his brother's arms,
But calmly gave his message from the King —
Of amnesty and pardon for the brave ;

Yet, once deliver'd of the weighty task,
He threw his arms around his brother's neck;
And both withdrew to where they were alone
For tender talk and interchange of love:
Tho' speech came slowly — choked at first with
        tears.
And then Hermenegild pleaded well and long
How just his cause; with what extreme of pain
The conflict had been forced upon his heart —
A heart which ever had excused the King,
Believing him tongue-lash'd and play'd upon
By one whom both could value at her worth.

" Ah, could our noble mother but have liv'd!
Thou hast not yet forgotten her, I trow ? "
" Nor ever shall," quoth Reccared.   " To me
Her memory has been a guiding star."
" Then what of the faith which made her very
        life ?
Hast thou no wish to share it — and with me ?
Of all things precious Truth Divine is first."
" Yes, dearest brother: and the hope is mine
That we shall all erelong — the King himself,
And this fair Spain of ours from North to South —
Hold but one creed, in one pure worship join.

For did not the late Council shape decrees
With view to union?   Surely, thou hast heard?"

" Ay, heard and understood.   Be not deceiv'd,
Sweet brother.   Truth admits no compromise.
That term of ' equal,' in the Arian sense,
Leaves Co-Eterne and Consubstantial out.
Were but our uncle, good Leander, here,
To show thee all the truth, as once to me
He show'd it!   But enough that thou dost wish
To know it, as I doubt not.   Search and pray.
And since in our dead mother thou hast found
A guiding star, and oft invokest her,
Think how much more a mother She must be
Whose Son is God, yet we Her children too.
Come, pray with me before Her image here,
That She may be indeed the morning star
Of perfect day for thee."

                              They knelt: and when
With radiant face Hermenegild arose,
He blithely said: " The King would have me
        come
And sue for pardon and the kiss of peace?
'Tis well.   I own whatever fault be mine
Of rashness, haste, or anger.   Let us go."

VI

The King had conquer'd; and could well afford
To show himself magnanimously royal.
His better nature triumph'd for the nonce.
So, when his son bent humbly at his feet
In painful silence, finding naught to say,
Leovigild uprais'd him, kiss'd his cheek,
And motion'd to a throne upon his right.
"Sit there, my son — still Andalusia's Prince.
A lesson thou hast learnt has cost thee dear:
But not in vain, if duly stored in mind.
And now we know thy prowess, we avow
'Tis worthy of thy line.   If thou didst fail,
'Twas not for lack of military skill,
Nor yet from want of numbers or of arms:
But we, to save a fratricidal strife,
Used means 'gainst which thy subjects were not
          proof.
Dishonorable means they else had been,
But for averting grievous waste of blood.

"Come with us now, my son, to Hispalis.
Let thine own capital receive thee back
With joy and promise of enduring peace.
We will disband the army, save a guard

Befitting our estate, and one to march
With thy young brother to his Northern home."

All this was smooth as some deep river's flow.
No word of faith, no hint of change, no sign
Of former wrath at pertinacious creed.
" If smooth the surface, dark the depths, I ween,"
Sigh'd poor Hermenegild. " The King's design
I guess not; but await the will of God."
Nor bode he long expectant.   Came an hour
Of pompous entry with the victor King
Between the wide-flung gates of Hispalis:
And seem'd he then not vanquish'd, not de-
    spoil'd;
But rescued by a father's stronger arm
From wild fanatical folly, and restored
To his forgiving subjects, sane and crown'd.
But passed the day; and came another hour,
When solemn re-instatement was to make
The Prince once more vice-regent of the King.
The herald-summon'd city gazed and heard.

" Be 't known to all," said then Leovigild,
" That what our son proclaim'd of liberty
For creed and worship we ourself confirm.

Not changed the State religion, she extends
The hand of friendship to the rival Church,
Inviting explanations with a view
To restful union.   Prince Hermenegild,
As our vice-regent, needs must hold and show
True fealty to the Church of King and State:
But will, with warmest advocacy, strive,
And zeal that cannot fail, to bring about
The wish'd conciliation."
                    Thus, at last,
Transparent shone the river's depths beneath
The smooth and treacherous surface.   Wisely
    plann'd
Thy scheme, O crafty one, hadst had a son
Of other mould — of faithless mother born:
A son to whom the sacredness of truth
Had been as nothing; who had valued more
An earthly kingdom than a crown in Heaven.
Not such a son Hermenegild to thee,
Not such a prince for subjects to his charge
Entrusted.
            See, he rises — pale, but calm:
No panic at heart; no quaver in the voice
Which answers the King's challenge, clear and
    strong.

"I stand this day before you, O my friends,
Restor'd, his gracious Majesty hath said,
To his, my father's, favor, and to yours.
I own, most humbly, to impetuous moods —
To rashness, if you will — to much that youth
Must plead excuse for.   But have never been
A conscious traitor to my country's weal;
Nor yet to Truth Divine, as known to me.
To see our Spain united in one faith,
One worship, is a boon I daily ask
From Him whose power alone can compass it.
But vainly will the State Church reach a hand,
Or make concessions, to a rival creed;
While holding back submission to the Chair
Of Peter, and acceptance unreserv'd
Of Catholic Apostolic Roman faith.

"And since that faith, once known and once
      receiv'd,
Can never be abandon'd without sin
Which damns the soul and rarely fails to drag
The traitor down to everlasting Hell
(For rarely doth repentance follow it);
And since, as well ye know, that faith is mine: —
I therefore turn me to the King, my sire,

In presence of you all, and beg resign
My share of throne and sceptre; beg to go
An exile from my native land and dwell
With wife and child where I may pray in peace —
A right denied me here."

But on the King
An evil spirit fell, as erst on Saul
When God had left him.

"Be it so!" he cried.
"Resign thou shalt.   Arrest him, men at arms!
Tear off his royal robes, and let him stand
A common clown — no longer son of ours
Before the multitude that hail'd him Prince!
And guard him well.   To-morrow we pronounce
His sentence.   Go, good people, to your homes."

He waited not the morrow.   That day's night
In Hispalis' strong tower a captive lay
The princely victim of a father's wrath.

VII

Such heresy's accursèd hate of truth.
'Twas ever so, since Cain his brother slew —
Cain the first heretic.   But not as yet

Had this despotic father in his heart
The thought of murder.   Winter setting in,
He fondly deem'd a spell of fetter'd limbs,
And cold stone walls, and bed of hardest floor,
With beggar's fare, and ghastly solitude,
Best argument for one in palace rear'd
And son of proud Leovigild.
                        " A month,"
Quoth he to favor'd courtier, " ay, a month
Will bring him to his senses and his knees.
But we will hold the reins in Hispalis
The winter thro', if need be.   We have sent
To have the Queen rejoin us."
                          But the Prince,
A true confessor, gloried in his bonds,
And pray'd that only death might set him free.
Tho' daily his sweet wife and blooming boy
Came vividly before him, he had learnt
So well to love in God the gifts of God,
That thought of ne'er beholding them again
On earth was lost in certain hope of Heaven,
Where meetings come, but partings never-
    more.
Leander's promise — might it not receive
Its long-delay'd fulfilment after death?

Came no Leander now; but Arian priest,
Or prelate, to essay their subtlest art;
Returning baffled to the baffled King.
One month, another; then a fourth, a fifth;
Till his sire marvell'd that he still liv'd on,
Ev'n more than at his obstinate contempt —
For such faith's constancy in alien eyes.
'Twas little guess'd that good Leander's prayer,
And pure Ingunda's, blended with his own
To form the triple cord unbreakable
Which bound both soul and body with its strength.

But now Gosvinda and the Arian Church,
Who long had counsell'd death, as treason's due,
So wrought upon Leovigild's hurt pride,
That, silencing the father's heart in him,
With sudden swerve he yielded to their will.

'Twas Passion-tide: and well Hermenegild
Kept consort with his agonizing Lord,
As, scene by scene, the wondrous story brought
Fresh comfort to his soul.   For he had conn'd
That story o'er and o'er, nor other page
Than memory's needed now.
                              And much he dwelt

On Jesus crown'd, as a mock king, with thorns —
Tho' King of kings : derided as a fool,
Tho' Infinite Wisdom : a deceiver call'd,
Tho' Truth itself : and unto that dear Lord
Offer'd in turn his own discrowning — all
That he had borne for " witness to the truth."
And this with deepest thankfulness and joy
That Christ had doled him such a share of woe.

Now Holy Week began its stately march.
He follow'd day by day, and step for step.
Spy-Wednesday came, the traitor Judas' day.
Ah, how he blest God's grace and mercy then,
Had kept him from betraying Christ anew !
And lo, the final test, the last assault,
Was drawing onward with the morrow's night.

In those far times, the Church kept Holy Week
As erst among the catacombs of Rome :
Her Arian rival aping her in this.
The awful night which saw our dearest Lord
Bequeath His Body and Blood, His very Self,
As Eucharistic Sacrifice and Food,
Was not forestall'd, but spent in order due.

Hermenegild had wakefully arrived
The midnight hour in contemplation sweet,
When suddenly made entrance to his cell
An Arian bishop, with attendant lights,
Bearing a silver vessel, which he held
Before his breast : and thus began his say.

" My Prince, thy father, our most gracious
    King,
Distressfully entreats thee put an end
To this unnatural and bootless strife,
Which harrows up his own heart, even as thine.
He has receiv'd to-night our common Christ ;
And bids his servant, my unworthiness,
Deliver the same Bread of Life to thee.
Receive it, and be free."
                " Ay, free forsooth
With fallen Peter !   Give the traitor's kiss,
And end despairing !   Prithee tell the King
To dream no more of any change in me."

" Then dread, young man, the vengeance long
    delay'd
Which waits upon high treason."

But the Prince
Slept soundly when Hell's minister had gone.
And woke to spend the Crucifixion day
In tenderest union with his Saviour-Lord.

VIII

" Now there was darkness over all the land
From sixth hour unto ninth." Amid these
    hours,
It seem'd to Prince Hermenegild he knelt
On Calvary's very top, and close to the Cross.

Faith changed to vision : for he saw and heard :
And lo, at heart of the darkness there was light !
Our Dolorous Lady " turn'd her pitying eyes,"
And placed a beauteous hand upon his head :
Then to Her Son Divine, whose Cross-stretch'd
    form
Hung " white and ruddy," she presented him
As chosen for the Choir of Martyrdom :
And He, the King of Martyrs, She, the Queen,
Accepted there the generous sacrifice.

But past the Friday peacefully withal ;
Nor ruffian blow, nor fell, intruding voice.

So that our hero moan'd that he survived
His Master's death-day : yet, with perfect trust,
Look'd wistfully for Easter's nearing morn
As promised hour of triumph — nor in vain.

The calm of Holy Saturday — its sense
Of rest with Jesus in His Sabbath-tomb —
Seem'd linger most unwontedly.   With night,
The Church began her long and solemn rites
That led up to the Mass of Easter's dawn.

Behold where sweet Ingunda makes her prayer—
Beside her sleeping boy !   The midnight hour
Has struck ; and she must robe herself and go
Into the great cathedral for the Mass.
Her thoughts have been with Mary, Mother of
      God,
In that entrancèd vigil which awoke
To sight of Jesus risen and glorified.
And is not *she* expectant ?   She has learnt,
Thro' kind Leander, how her valiant Prince
Had vanquish'd been by gold and treachery :
And how the King had reinstated him
With test severest of a constant faith.
Then came the father's wrath, the son's arrest ;

And how, in Hispalis' strong castle bound,
The prisoner so had balk'd the royal scheme,
That seem'd it likeliest the wearied King
Would send him forth, a banish'd man — but
      free
To fly to her, if never to return.
'Twas this she pray'd for, till the latest word,
Which came with Passion-tide.
                                        Leander wrote : —
" A change, my daughter — sudden, dark, and
      fell —
Has clouded o'er the counsels of the King.
Prepare thee — for it seems the will of God —
To have thy husband win the martyr's palm !
I well believe that Easter morn I saw,
When thou shouldst hail him victor from the
      fight,
Is now arriving.   It has tarried long.
Fear nothing.   God will hold thee with a
      grace —
A strength that faileth not."
                                        And from that hour
A wondrous grace encompass'd and sustain'd
This gentle soul to meet the will of God
Not only with submission, but with joy.

And now, as she arises from her prayer
To robe and pass to Mass, she does not see
Her heart's belovèd kneeling in his cell;
Nor the hard soldier, who, intruding, cries
" I execute the sentence of the King!" —
And lifts an axe, and cleaves him thro' the
    brain.

She sees not this : but lo, her room is fill'd
With sudden light from other world than ours!
And in that light she sees our Lady sweet
Smiling upon her, and, with gracious hand,
Giving her back her lost Hermenegild
(Now lost no longer, but her own forever),
A martyr crown'd: " crown'd victor from the
    fight" —
For Christ's dear Godhead and His Spouse the
    Church.

O bliss unutterable!   Where the heart
Of mortal wife could hold it all and live ?
Ingunda's broke — burst with its ecstasy ;
And her pure soul, in Mary's bosom borne,
To Jesus' feet was carried where He sits
At God's right hand, Saviour and Judge of all.

And He receiv'd it from His Mother's love,
And welcom'd it to Heav'n, and gave it right
To wear with its dear spouse the martyr's crown.

IX

To Sigisbert first, the father kind and true,
Whose Easter joy his daughter's sudden death
Had marr'd exceedingly, the Blessèd Pair
Reveal'd themselves in light.
                    " We leave to thee
Our orphan boy, Theodoric, gift of God,"
Ingunda said.   " Thou who hast ever been
A father true to me, be now as true
A father to him.   Watch o'er his youthful days,
And we will watch o'er thee.   Take special heed
To train him in the faith.   We know not yet
What God may have in store for him ; but this
We promise — that our prayer shall go with
        thine
For him, nor less for thee and all thou lov'st,
So thou be faithful to this trust."
                    " Amen ! "
Made answer Sigisbert, now full of joy :
And well he kept his promise.

Next they came
To where Leovigild, in gloom and dread,
Paced silent, lamp-lit halls in Hispalis.
'Twas night, but sleep forsook the guilty King.
Astonish'd, terrified, he struck his breast
And sank upon his knees, when issued forth
From dim-lit solitude the beauteous forms.
Then spoke Hermenegild :

" Bethink thee not
We come as ministers of wrath divine,
O blinded instrument of highest good !
We rather come to thank thee for our crown
Of martyrdom, and offer thee from God
A final grace of penance and of faith.

" The Lord Christ bids thee know His Catholic
    Church
Is Roman — the One Shepherd's only fold.
That He, the Word, is very God of God
Begotten ; Consubstantial, Co-Eterne
With the Almighty Father ; and made Flesh
Of Mother Ever-Virgin.   That the sect
To which thou cleavest blasphemously dares
Dissolve the Triune Godhead ; and has reft
Its duped adherents of the New Birth's grace,

By vitiated form.   Alas, poor King,
No faith is thine, no priest, no sacrament !
But thou art still my father, and I love
Thy soul more dearly now than when my own
Was clad in mortal garb.   Do penance, then,
My father.   Send for good Leander: learn
What he shall teach; and be baptized; and
    bring
Dear Reccared, and all our kith and kin,
And all the Visigoth portion of our Spain,
Back to the One True Fold.   Thy penance this.

" Thou needest fear no more Gosvinda's taunts,
In yonder chamber lies her lifeless face,
Her spirit down in Hell.   God's justice struck —
After long tarrying.   Nor hast aught to dread
From Arian malice, so thou use the power
Which God shall give thee.   We will ever pray,
And watch until we welcome thee above."

Here vanish'd from his eyes the Blessèd Pair;
And all seem'd darkness round him as he groped
His way to the royal chamber, there to find
Gosvinda black in death, as tho' a fiend
Had strangled her.

                      With morning he dispatch'd
A courier in hot haste to Corduba;
And one to Reccared's capital; resolv'd
To do at least a part — the greater part —
Of his dead son's injunction.   For himself,
Tho' now no more a heretic in will,
But owning the full truth, and scornfully
Repelling priest or prelate of the sect,
He fail'd to pray and humble his proud heart,
And trust the promised mercy.

                              When arrived
Leander, full of peace and holy joy —
He, too, had seen the Blessèd Pair, and heard
From them God's gracious offer to the King —
Leovigild receiv'd him wearily,
As part of a cause had triumph'd by defeat;
And treated him with deferential awe;
But gave no sign of hopeful penitence.
The saint saw thro' the King's unhappy mind,
And strove to rouse his hope, and make him own
His case a visible instance of God's ways
Of overruling evil unto good.

" Give God the glory, Sire.   Confess how vain,
How foolish, 'tis, in sooth, to plot and plan

Against His wisdom, or to lift a hand
To overthrow His purpose.   Thou, my liege,
Didst act, like Saul of Tarsus, blindly then.
But now a blessèd grace has brought thee light,
And made truth clear as day.   Thou needst
    not ask
' Lord, what wilt have me do ? ' for I am here
To tell thee.   But repent with contrite heart,
And be baptized, and wash thy sins away.
Then Faith divine, with Hope and Charity,
Will make thee a new man — a son of God."

" Thy words are good, lord bishop.   Let it
    keep —
This question — for the present.   We have sent
For Reccared, our sole successor now,
To place him in thy charge.   Do thou instruct,
Baptize, and seal him in the Catholic faith.
Our trust that his will one day be the power,
Denied to us, of bringing back our land
To Roman unity.   So grant it God ! "

Thus Reccared "the Catholic" took the throne;
Whose reign of triumph forms a glorious page
In Spain's long annals.   But his hapless sire

Liv'd not to share his victory.   Dragg'd him
   down
A broken (ah, but not a contrite!) heart.
Unchristen'd, unabsolv'd — tho' not unmourn'd,
Nor yet unpray'd for — soon he sank and died,
And went to Judgment in his proud despair.

But thou, my hero, Saint Hermenegild,
Whose precious death restor'd thy country's
   faith,
Pray for the minstrel who has thus presumed
To sing thy story!   Help him to be brave
And love the Cross, O Passion Flower of Spain!

St. Paul's Monastery,
Pittsburgh, Pa.
Octave of the Solemn Commemoration of the Passion,
1896.

Electrotyped by J. S. Cushing & Co., Norwood, Mass.

Printed by Benziger Brothers, New York.